Bus Services Act 2017

CHAPTER 21

Explanatory Notes are available separately

GRAN*GIS* UK Publishing

Adapted and published by GRANGIS (Grand Register Library).
Online: www.grangis.com
E-mail: contact@grangis.com

In this version:
ISBN: 979-8-88559-007-5

Note: This is the original version (as it was originally enacted). Title, sub-title and the generated date is as marked on the pages.

Bus Services Act 2017

CHAPTER 21

BUS SERVICES ACT 2017

Bus Services Act 2017

2017 CHAPTER 21

An Act to make provision about bus services; and for connected purposes. [27th April 2017]

BE IT ENACTED by the Queen's most Excellent Majesty, by and with the advice and consent of the Lords Spiritual and Temporal, and Commons, in this present Parliament assembled, and by the authority of the same, as follows:—

Advanced quality partnership schemes

1 Advanced quality partnership schemes

In Part 2 of the Transport Act 2000 (local transport), after section 113B insert—

"Bus services: advanced quality partnership schemes

113C Advanced quality partnership schemes

(1) A local transport authority whose area is in England, or two or more such authorities acting jointly, may make an advanced quality partnership scheme if they are satisfied that the scheme will contribute to the implementation of their local transport policies.

(2) An advanced quality partnership scheme is—

(a) a scheme falling within subsection (3) or (4), or

(b) a scheme falling within both subsection (3) and subsection (4).

(3) A scheme falls within this subsection if it is a scheme under which—

(a) the authority or authorities provide particular facilities in the whole or part of their area, or combined area, and

(b) operators of local services who wish to use those facilities must undertake to provide local services of a particular standard when using them.

(4) A scheme falls within this subsection if it is a scheme under which—

(a) the authority or authorities take particular measures in relation to routes in the whole or part of their area, or combined area, that are served, or proposed to be served, by local services, and

(b) operators of local services who wish to provide local services with stopping places on those routes must undertake to provide local services of a particular standard when providing such local services on those routes.

(5) A scheme may not be made unless the authority or authorities are satisfied that—

(a) the steps to be taken by the authority or authorities under the scheme, and

(b) the provision of local services of the standard or standards required by undertakings given under the scheme,

are likely to achieve one or more of the outcomes described in subsection (6) in relation to the whole or part of their area, or combined area.

(6) The outcomes mentioned in subsection (5) are—

(a) an improvement in the quality of local services that benefits persons using those services;

(b) a reduction or limitation of traffic congestion, noise or air pollution;

(c) an increase in the use of local services or an end to, or a reduction in, a decline in the use of local services.

(7) An advanced quality partnership scheme may not be made unless the authority or authorities have complied with the notice and consultation requirements imposed by section 113G.

(8) The power to make an advanced quality partnership scheme includes power to provide for—

(a) different facilities to be provided under the scheme,

(b) different measures to be taken under the scheme, or

(c) different standards of services to be provided under the scheme,

as from different dates after the scheme comes into operation.

(9) An advanced quality partnership scheme must include a description of the authority's or authorities' plans for consulting such organisations appearing to the authority or authorities to be representative of users of local services as they think fit in order to seek their views on how well the scheme is working.

(10) In carrying out their functions under this Part in relation to advanced quality partnership schemes, local transport authorities whose areas are in England must co-operate with one another.

(11) In considering whether to make an advanced quality partnership scheme, a local transport authority must have regard to the desirability, in appropriate cases, of making a scheme jointly with another such authority.

113D Advanced quality partnership schemes: registration restrictions

(1) If the authority or authorities making an advanced quality partnership scheme consider that it is necessary or expedient for any restrictions to be imposed on the registration of—

(a) any local services, or

(b) any local services of a particular description,

they may impose those restrictions ("registration restrictions") by specifying or describing them in the scheme.

(2) Any restrictions so imposed must be for the purpose of preventing or restricting—

(a) the provision of local services, or

(b) the variation or withdrawal of local services,

in cases where the authority or authorities consider that any such provision, or (as the case may be) variation or withdrawal, of services might be detrimental to the provision of services under the scheme.

(3) Where a scheme includes any registration restrictions by virtue of subsection (1), it must also specify the criteria ("registration criteria") by reference to which a traffic commissioner is to decide whether or not to accept an application for registration.

(4) In this section "registration", in relation to any service—

(a) means registration of prescribed particulars of the service under section 6 of the Transport Act 1985 (registration of local services), and

(b) includes a reference to the variation or cancellation of any such registration.

113E Advanced quality partnership schemes: facilities, measures and standards

(1) The facilities which may be specified in an advanced quality partnership scheme—

(a) must be facilities provided at specific locations along routes served, or proposed to be served, by local services within the area to which the scheme relates, or facilities which are ancillary to such facilities, but

(b) may not be facilities which are required to be provided as a result of section 139 or 140.

(2) The measures which may be specified in a scheme—

(a) must be measures taken for the purpose of—

(i) increasing the use of local services serving the routes to which the measures relate or ending or reducing a decline in the use of such services, or

(ii) improving the quality of local services serving the routes to which the measures relate, but

(b) may not include the provision of—

(i) facilities falling within subsection (1)(a), or

(ii) facilities which are required to be provided as a result of section 139 or 140.

(3) The Secretary of State may by regulations make further provision about the measures which may or may not be specified in a scheme.

(4) The standard of services which may be specified in a scheme includes—

(a) requirements which the vehicles being used to provide the services must meet, including requirements about emissions or types of fuel or power, and

(b) requirements as to frequency or timing of the services,

but the specification of any such requirements is not to prevent operators from providing services in excess of those requirements.

(5) The standard of services which may be specified in a scheme may also include—

(a) requirements as to the maximum fares that may be charged for particular journeys, or for journeys of particular descriptions, on services to which the scheme applies,

(b) requirements as to the ways in which passengers may pay for journeys,

(c) requirements about providing information to the public about local services or particular descriptions of local services, and

(d) requirements as to the publicising of local services, fares or ticketing arrangements or particular descriptions of local services, fares or ticketing arrangements.

(6) Requirements under subsection (5)(b), (c) and (d) may include requirements for operators of local services to co-operate with one another.

(7) A scheme may include a requirement falling within subsection (4)(b) or (5)(a) only if there are no admissible objections to the requirement from relevant operators.

(8) A scheme may include a requirement falling within subsection (4)(a) or (5)(b) that relates to an undertaking that would fall to be given under section 113C(4)(b) only if there are no admissible objections to the requirement from relevant operators.

(9) Section 113N(3) to (8) makes further provision with respect to schemes which include the requirements referred to in subsections (7) and (8).

113F Advanced quality partnership schemes: traffic regulation orders

(1) If the provision of any of the facilities or taking of any of the measures specified in an advanced quality partnership scheme requires the making of a traffic regulation order in respect of a road or other place in a metropolitan district (other than a road for which the Secretary of State is the traffic authority), the scheme may not be made unless it is made by—

(a) the local transport authority or authorities, and

(b) the metropolitan district council for the district,

acting jointly.

(2) If the provision of any of the facilities or taking of any of the measures specified in an advanced quality partnership scheme requires the making of a traffic regulation order in respect of a road for which the Secretary of State is the traffic authority, the scheme may not be made unless it is made by—

(a) the local transport authority or authorities, and

(b) the Secretary of State,

acting jointly.

(3) Where subsection (1) or (2) applies so that a metropolitan district council or the Secretary of State is a maker of the scheme, then (subject to section 113M) the relevant references to the authority or authorities include (as well as the local transport authority or authorities)—

(a) the metropolitan district council, or

(b) the Secretary of State.

(4) For the purpose of subsection (3) the relevant references are those in—

(a) section 113C(3), (4), (5)(a) and (7), and

(b) sections 113G to 113L,

and paragraph 27(2A) of Schedule 9 to the Road Traffic Regulation Act 1984.

113G Notice and consultation requirements

(1) If an authority or authorities propose to make an advanced quality partnership scheme, they must give notice of the proposed scheme in such manner as they consider appropriate for drawing it to the attention of persons in the area to which it relates.

(2) The notice must either contain full details of—

(a) any facilities specified in the scheme,

(b) any measures specified in the scheme,

(c) the standards of services specified in the scheme,

(d) any registration restrictions and registration criteria specified in the scheme, and

(e) the plans described in the scheme for consulting in order to seek views on how well the scheme is working,

or state where such details may be inspected.

(3) After giving notice of the proposed scheme, the authority or authorities must consult—

(a) all operators of local services who would, in the opinion of the authority or authorities, be affected by it,

(b) such organisations appearing to the authority or authorities to be representative of users of local services as they think fit,

(c) any other relevant local authority any part of whose area would, in the opinion of the authority or authorities, be affected by it,

(d) a traffic commissioner,

(e) the chief officer of police for each police area covering the whole or part of that area,

(f) the Passengers' Council,

(g) the Competition and Markets Authority, and

(h) such other persons as the authority or authorities think fit.

(4) For the purpose of subsection (3)(c) the following are relevant local authorities—

(a) local transport authorities,

(b) district councils in England,

(c) National Park authorities,

(d) the Broads Authority,

(e) London transport authorities, and

(f) councils in Scotland.

113H Making of scheme

(1) If, after taking the steps described in section 113G, an authority or authorities decide that it is appropriate to make the advanced quality partnership scheme, they may make it as proposed or with modifications.

(2) The scheme must specify each of the following—

(a) any facilities to be provided under it by the authority or authorities,

(b) any measures to be taken under it by the authority or authorities and the routes to which they relate,

(c) the standards of services to be provided under it by operators of local services in accordance with their undertakings given in relation to facilities or measures to be provided or taken under the scheme,

(d) any registration restrictions imposed by it and any registration criteria specified in it,

(e) the date on which it is to come into operation,

(f) the period for which it is to remain in operation, which must not be less than five years, and

(g) if—

(i) any facilities are to be provided under the scheme,

(ii) any measures are to be taken under the scheme, or

(iii) any standards of services are to be provided under the scheme,

as from a date after the scheme comes into operation, the date as from which they are to be so provided or taken.

(3) The scheme may provide that—

(a) local services specified in it, or

(b) local services of a class specified in it,

are to be excluded from the scheme, subject to such conditions (if any) as may be specified in it.

(4) The date as from which any particular facilities are to be provided, any particular measures are to be taken, or any services of a particular standard are to be provided, must not be earlier than—

(a) in the case of facilities or measures, the latest of dates A to C (see subsections (6) to (8)), and

(b) in the case of services, the later of dates A and D (see subsections (6) and (9)),

unless the case falls within subsection (5).

(5) If under the scheme—

(a) particular facilities are to be provided or particular measures are to be taken by the authority or authorities, and

(b) as from the date by which the facilities are to be provided or the measures are to be taken, services of a particular standard are to be provided by operators of local services when using the facilities or when providing local services with stopping places on routes to which the measures relate,

the date as from which the facilities are to be provided or the measures are to be taken (and as from which the services are to be provided) must not be earlier than the latest of dates A to D.

(6) Date A is the date 3 months after the date on which the scheme is made.

(7) Date B is the date by which, in the opinion of the authority or authorities, it will be reasonably practicable for the authority or authorities to provide the facilities or take the measures.

(8) Date C is the date 3 months after—

(a) the date on which any traffic regulation order required for the provision of any of the facilities or taking of any of the measures is made, or

(b) if more than one such order is required for the provision of the facilities or the taking of the measures, the date on which the last of them is made.

(9) Date D is the date by which, in the opinion of the authority or authorities, it will be reasonably practicable for operators of local services to provide services of the particular standard.

(10) Not later than 14 days after the date on which the scheme is made, the authority or authorities must give notice of the making of the scheme—

(a) in such manner as they consider appropriate for drawing it to the attention of persons in the area to which it relates,

(b) to all operators of local services who would, in their opinion, be affected by the scheme, and

(c) to a traffic commissioner.

(11) The notice must—

(a) either contain full details of the scheme or state where such details may be inspected, and

(b) if the scheme made is a modified version of that proposed, state that fact.

113I Postponement of scheme or of provision of particular facilities, taking of particular measures or provision of particular standards of service

(1) If it appears to the authority or authorities appropriate to do so, they may decide that any of the dates specified in subsection (3) shall be postponed by such period as they think fit.

(2) A date may not be postponed under subsection (1) by a period or periods which in total exceed 12 months.

(3) The dates are—

(a) the date on which the scheme is to come into operation,

(b) the date as from which any particular facilities are to be provided under the scheme,

(c) the date as from which any particular measures are to be taken under the scheme, and

(d) the date as from which any particular services are to be provided to a particular standard under the scheme.

(4) Before making such a decision the authority or authorities must consult all operators of local services who would, in their opinion, be affected by the scheme.

(5) Not later than 14 days after the date on which any such decision is made they must give notice of the decision—

(a) in such manner as they consider appropriate for drawing it to the attention of persons in the area to which it relates,

(b) to all operators of local services who would, in their opinion, be affected by the scheme, and

(c) to a traffic commissioner.

113J Effect of scheme

(1) The authority or authorities must—

(a) provide each of the specified facilities or take each of the specified measures not later than the date specified for it to be provided or taken under the scheme, and

(b) continue to provide the facilities or keep the measures in effect throughout the remainder of the period for which the scheme is in operation.

(2) But subsection (1) does not apply in relation to any period during which the authority or authorities are temporarily unable to provide the facilities or take the measures or keep the measures in effect owing to circumstances beyond their control.

(3) Nor does it apply in the case of the Secretary of State if the Secretary of State is unable to provide the facilities or take the measures or keep the measures in effect owing to the variation or revocation of a traffic regulation order.

(4) The operator of a local service may not use facilities provided under an advanced quality partnership scheme unless—

(a) the operator has given a written undertaking to a traffic commissioner that, when using the facilities on any date, the operator will provide the service to the standard specified in the scheme that is relevant to the use of those facilities on that date, and

(b) the operator provides the service to that standard when using the facilities, except in relation to any period during which the operator is temporarily unable to do so owing to circumstances beyond the operator's control.

(5) Where a measure has been taken under an advanced quality partnership scheme, the operator of a local service may not use a stopping place on a route to which that measure relates unless—

(a) the operator has given a written undertaking to a traffic commissioner that, when using such a stopping place on any date, the operator will provide the service to the standard specified in the scheme that is relevant to the use of such a stopping place on that date, and

(b) the operator provides the service to that standard when using such a stopping place, except in relation to any period during which the operator is temporarily unable to do so owing to circumstances beyond the operator's control.

(6) But subsections (4) and (5) do not apply in relation to services which are excluded from the scheme as a result of any provision of the scheme made in accordance with section 113H(3).

(7) Where the exclusion of a local service from the scheme is made subject to conditions as a result of such a provision, those conditions are to be treated, during any period in which the scheme is in operation, as if they were prescribed particulars of the service concerned registered under section 6 of the Transport Act 1985 (registration of local services).

113K Regulations about schemes involving existing facilities or measures which are already in effect

(1) The Secretary of State may by regulations make provision about the specifying in advanced quality partnership schemes of—

(a) facilities which are already being provided before the schemes are proposed ("existing facilities"), and

(b) measures which are already in effect before the schemes are proposed ("existing measures").

(2) The regulations may in particular—

(a) provide that existing facilities may not be specified if they were being provided before a date prescribed by, or determined in accordance with, the regulations,

(b) provide that existing measures may not be specified if they were in effect before such a date,

(c) provide that—

(i) particular existing facilities or classes of existing facilities, or

(ii) particular existing measures or classes of existing measures,

may not be specified (whenever they were first provided or taken),

(d) provide that—

(i) particular existing facilities or classes of existing facilities, or

(ii) particular existing measures or classes of existing measures,

may be specified only in circumstances prescribed by the regulations,

(e) provide that, in circumstances prescribed by the regulations—

(i) particular existing facilities or classes of existing facilities, or

(ii) particular existing measures or classes of existing measures, may be specified only with the consent of a person prescribed by, or determined in accordance with, the regulations, and

(f) make provision modifying any provision of sections 113G to 113I in relation to schemes which specify existing facilities or existing measures.

113L Variation or revocation of schemes

(1) The authority or authorities who made an advanced quality partnership scheme may vary the scheme if they decide that it is appropriate to do so.

(2) The authority or authorities who made a scheme may revoke it before the end of the period for which it would otherwise remain in operation if all persons who have given an undertaking to provide a service to the standard specified in the scheme consent to the revocation of the scheme; and such consent must not be unreasonably withheld.

(3) If the variation of a scheme under subsection (1) would require the making of a traffic regulation order, the variation is subject to the same procedure as the making of a scheme.

(4) Any other variation of a scheme under subsection (1), or the revocation of a scheme under subsection (2), is subject to that procedure, except to the extent that the procedure is modified by regulations made under section 113N.

113M Variation: supplementary

(1) The relevant references to the authority or authorities in relation to an advanced quality partnership scheme—

(a) include a local transport authority if it has been varied so that it relates to that authority's area, but

(b) do not include a local transport authority if it has been varied so that it no longer relates to that authority's area.

(2) But if (although the scheme does not relate to a local transport authority's area) it would do by reason of a proposed variation, those references (apart from those in section 113J) include that authority.

(3) The relevant references (apart from those in section 113C(1) and in the words before paragraph (a) of section 113C(5)) to the authority or authorities in relation to an advanced quality partnership scheme—

(a) include a traffic regulation authority if it has been varied so that it specifies traffic regulation facilities or traffic regulation measures, but

(b) do not include a traffic regulation authority if it has been varied so that it no longer specifies such facilities or measures.

(4) But if (although the scheme does not specify facilities which are traffic regulation facilities in relation to a traffic regulation authority or measures which are traffic regulation measures in relation to a traffic regulation authority) it would do by reason of a proposed variation, those references (apart from those in section 113J) include that authority.

(5) And if (although the scheme specifies facilities which are traffic regulation facilities in relation to a traffic regulation authority or measures which are traffic regulation measures in relation to a traffic regulation authority)—

(a) the traffic regulation order, or (where more than one) each of the traffic regulation orders, required to be made by that authority for the provision of those facilities or the taking of those measures has been revoked, and

(b) the scheme is proposed to be varied (but not so that it specifies other facilities which are traffic regulation facilities in relation to that authority or other measures which are traffic regulation measures in relation to that authority),

the relevant references (apart from those in section 113J) do not include that authority.

(6) For the purposes of this section the relevant references are those in—

(a) section 113C(1) to (7),

(b) section 113D, and

(c) sections 113G to 113L,

and paragraph 27(2A) of Schedule 9 to the Road Traffic Regulation Act 1984.

(7) In this section "traffic regulation authority" means—

(a) a metropolitan district council, or

(b) the Secretary of State.

(8) For the purposes of this section—

(a) facilities are traffic regulation facilities, in relation to a traffic regulation authority and an advanced quality partnership scheme, if that authority was required to be a maker of the scheme because it originally specified those facilities or would have been required to be a maker of it had it done so;

(b) measures are traffic regulation measures, in relation to a traffic regulation authority and an advanced quality partnership scheme, if that authority was required to be a maker of the scheme because it originally specified those measures or would have been required to be a maker of it had it done so.

113N Regulations about schemes

(1) The Secretary of State may by regulations make further provision with respect to—

(a) the procedure to be followed when making, varying or revoking advanced quality partnership schemes,

(b) the content or operation of schemes which include—

(i) a requirement falling within section 113E(4)(b) or (5)(a), or

(ii) a requirement falling within section 113E(4)(a) or (5)(b) relating to an undertaking that would fall to be given under section 113C(4)(b),

(c) the local services or classes of local services which must be, or may be, excluded from schemes,

(d) the conditions which must be, or may be, attached to such exclusions,

(e) the form and manner in which undertakings are to be given to a traffic commissioner in connection with schemes,

(f) the making of traffic regulation orders in connection with schemes, and

(g) such other incidental matters in connection with advanced quality partnership schemes as the Secretary of State thinks fit.

(2) The regulations may in particular make provision with respect to—

(a) giving notice of proposed schemes or proposed variations or revocation of schemes,

(b) objections to such proposals,

(c) the holding of inquiries or hearings into objections,

(d) modifications of such proposals,

(e) the form of schemes or variations, and

(f) giving notice of schemes which have been made or of the variation or revocation of schemes.

(3) As regards schemes which include or would include—

(a) a requirement described in subsection (1)(b)(i), or

(b) a requirement described in subsection (1)(b)(ii),

regulations under subsection (1)(a) or (b) may in particular make the provision referred to in subsection (4).

(4) The provision mentioned in subsection (3) is provision—

(a) for section 113E(7) or (8) not to apply in such circumstances as may be prescribed,

(b) in prescribed circumstances where such schemes, or any provisions of such schemes, are subject to postponement under section 113I, for any such requirement not to take effect unless prescribed conditions are satisfied,

(c) as to the meaning of "admissible objection" for the purposes of section 113E(7) and (8) and subsection (5)(b) of this section,

(d) as to the meaning of "relevant operator" for those purposes, and

(e) as to the determination of any question whether an objection is an admissible objection or an operator is a relevant operator.

(5) As regards schemes which include a requirement described in subsection (1)(b)(i), regulations under subsection (1)(b) may also make provision—

(a) requiring such schemes to include provision—

(i) as respects the setting of frequencies, timings or maximum fares to which the requirements relate,

(ii) for a minimum interval before any requirements as to frequencies, timings or maximum fares may next be reviewed,

(iii) for a maximum interval before any such requirements must next be reviewed,

(iv) as respects other circumstances in which any such requirements must or may be reviewed, and

(v) as respects revision of any such requirements after a review, and

(b) for any requirement as to frequencies, timings or maximum fares to be revised only if there are no admissible objections to the revision from relevant operators.

(6) The revision of requirements as to frequencies, timings or maximum fares under any provision included in a scheme by virtue of regulations under subsection (5)(a) is not to be regarded as a variation of the scheme for the purposes of section 113L (variation or revocation of schemes).

(7) Nothing in subsection (5) or (6) is to be taken to derogate from what may be done under or by virtue of section 113L.

(8) The provision that may be made by virtue of subsection (4)(e) includes provision for and in connection with—

(a) the appointment of a person ("an adjudicator") to make such a determination as is mentioned in that paragraph;

(b) the appointment of a person ("an assessor") to assist an adjudicator in considering any question which appears to arise in relation to such a determination;

(c) the payment—

(i) by the Secretary of State to an adjudicator, or

(ii) by the Secretary of State or an adjudicator to an assessor,

of such remuneration as may be determined by or in accordance with the regulations.

113O Guidance about schemes

(1) The Secretary of State may issue guidance concerning the carrying out by local transport authorities whose areas are in England and metropolitan district councils of their functions under this Part in relation to advanced quality partnership schemes.

(2) Those authorities and councils must have regard to any such guidance."

2 Further amendments

Schedule 1 contains further amendments relating to advanced quality partnership schemes.

3 Transitional provision

(1) Subsection (2) applies in relation to a quality partnership scheme under section 114 of the Transport Act 2000 that—

(a) is in operation, or made but not yet in operation, immediately before the commencement date, and

(b) at that time relates only to the areas of one or more local transport authorities in England.

(2) The scheme is to be treated from the commencement date as if it were an advanced quality partnership scheme that had been made under section 113C of the Transport Act 2000 (inserted by section 1).

(3) Subsection (4) applies in relation to a quality partnership scheme that, as varied under section 120 of the Transport Act 2000 after the commencement date, relates only to the areas of one or more local transport authorities in England.

(4) The scheme is to be treated from the date on which the scheme as varied comes into operation as if it were an advanced quality partnership scheme that had been made under section 113C of the Transport Act 2000.

(5) In this section "the commencement date" is the date on which section 1 comes into force for all purposes.

Franchising schemes

4 Franchising schemes

In Part 2 of the Transport Act 2000, after section 123 insert—

"Bus services: franchising schemes

123A Franchising schemes

(1) A franchising authority, or two or more franchising authorities acting jointly, may make a franchising scheme covering the whole or any part of their area, or their combined area.

(2) A franchising scheme may not be made unless the franchising authority or authorities have complied with the requirements in sections 123B to 123G.

(3) A franchising scheme is a scheme—

(a) under which the authority or authorities identify the local services that they consider appropriate to be provided in an area under local service contracts,

(b) by virtue of which those local services may only be provided in that area in accordance with local service contracts (subject to section 123O),

(c) by virtue of which the authority or authorities may grant service permits for other local services which have a stopping place in that area (subject to section 123H(5)), and

(d) under which the authority or authorities identify additional facilities that they consider appropriate to provide in that area.

(4) In this Part "franchising authority" means—

(a) a mayoral combined authority,

(b) a county council in England for an area for which there are district councils,

(c) a county council in England for an area for which there is no district council,

(d) a non-metropolitan district council for an area for which there is no county council,

(e) an Integrated Transport Authority for an integrated transport area in England, or

(f) a combined authority which is not a mayoral combined authority.

But each of paragraphs (b) to (f) has effect only if the Secretary of State by regulations so provides.

(5) In this Part "local service contract", in relation to a franchising scheme, means an agreement that complies with section 123K(1) to (3) under which—

(a) the franchising authority or authorities grant to another person the exclusive right to operate the local services to which the contract relates, and

(b) the person undertakes to provide the local services on such terms (including in particular as to frequency, fares and standard of service) as may be specified in the agreement.

(6) The terms as to standard of service that may be specified include terms about requirements which vehicles being used to provide the service must meet, including requirements about emissions or types of fuel or power.

(7) A local service contract may be made on terms which include provision for the making of payments by the authority or authorities to the person undertaking to provide the local service.

(8) Section 88(1) of the Transport Act 1985 (application to subsidy agreements of sections 89 to 92 of that Act) does not apply in relation to local service contracts.

(9) A franchising scheme must include a description of the franchising authority's or authorities' plans for consulting such organisations appearing to the authority or authorities to be representative of users of local services as they think fit in order to seek their views on how well the scheme is working.

(10) A franchising authority's functions under this Part in relation to a franchising scheme are excluded from the functions to which section 101(1)(b) of the Local Government Act 1972 applies, where the franchising authority is a local authority within the meaning of section 101 of the Local Government Act 1972.

123B Assessment of proposed scheme

(1) A franchising authority or authorities that propose to make a franchising scheme covering the whole or any part of their area, or combined area, must prepare an assessment of the proposed scheme.

(2) The assessment must—

(a) describe the effects that the proposed scheme is likely to produce, and

(b) compare making the proposed scheme to one or more other courses of action.

(3) The assessment must also include consideration of—

(a) whether the proposed scheme would contribute to the implementation of—

(i) the authority's or authorities' policies under section 108(1)(a), and

(ii) other policies affecting local services that the authority or authorities have adopted and published,

(b) whether the proposed scheme would contribute to the implementation by neighbouring relevant local authorities of—

(i) those authorities' policies under section 108(1)(a), and

(ii) other policies affecting local services that those authorities have adopted and published,

(c) how the authority or authorities would make and operate the proposed scheme,

(d) whether the authority or authorities would be able to afford to make and operate the scheme,

(e) whether the proposed scheme would represent value for money, and

(f) the extent to which the authority or authorities are likely to be able to secure that local services are operated under local service contracts.

(4) Subsections (2) and (3) do not prevent inclusion of other matters.

(5) The Secretary of State must issue guidance concerning the preparation of an assessment under this section, and that guidance may, in particular, include guidance about methods to be used when assessing a proposed scheme.

(6) Franchising authorities must have regard to any such guidance.

(7) In this section "relevant local authority" means—

(a) a local transport authority,

(b) a London transport authority, or

(c) a council in Scotland.

123C Consent of the Secretary of State and notice

(1) A franchising authority or authorities may not prepare an assessment of a proposed franchising scheme under section 123B unless the Secretary of State consents to their doing so.

(2) The Secretary of State's consent is not required if the proposed scheme relates only to—

(a) the area of a mayoral combined authority, or

(b) the combined area of two or more mayoral combined authorities.

(3) The Secretary of State must publish a notice of a consent given under this section.

(4) Before preparing an assessment of a proposed franchising scheme under section 123B, the authority or authorities must publish, in such manner as they consider appropriate, a notice stating that they intend to prepare such an assessment.

123D Audit

(1) If, after preparing an assessment of a proposed franchising scheme under section 123B, the authority or authorities wish to proceed with the proposed scheme, they must obtain a report from an independent auditor on that assessment.

(2) The auditor's report must state whether, in the opinion of the auditor—

(a) the information relied on by the authority or authorities in considering the matters referred to in section 123B(3)(d) or (e) is of sufficient quality,

(b) the analysis of that information in the assessment is of sufficient quality, and

(c) the authority or authorities had due regard to guidance issued under section 123B in preparing the assessment.

(3) The Secretary of State must issue guidance as to the matters to be taken into account by a franchising authority when selecting a person to act as an auditor.

(4) Franchising authorities must have regard to any such guidance.

(5) The Secretary of State must issue guidance concerning the matters to be taken into account by an auditor when forming an opinion as to whether the information relied on, and the analysis of that information, by an authority is of sufficient quality for the purposes of subsection (2).

(6) Auditors must have regard to any such guidance.

(7) For the purposes of this section an auditor is independent, in relation to an assessment of a proposed franchising scheme, if the person would not be disqualified from acting as local auditor of the accounts of the franchising authority, or any of the franchising authorities, under section 1214 of the Companies Act 2006 as substituted by paragraph 5 of Schedule 5 to the Local Audit and Accountability Act 2014.

(8) In this section "auditor" means a person eligible for appointment as a local auditor by virtue of Chapter 2 of Part 42 of the Companies Act 2006 as modified by Schedule 5 to the Local Audit and Accountability Act 2014.

123E Consultation

(1) This section applies if, after obtaining an auditor's report under section 123D, the authority or authorities wish to proceed with the proposed franchising scheme.

(2) The authority or authorities must—

(a) publish a consultation document relating to the proposed scheme (see section 123F),

(b) publish the assessment of the proposed scheme,

(c) publish the auditor's report on that assessment, and

(d) give notice of the proposed scheme in such manner as the authority or authorities consider appropriate for bringing it to the attention of persons in the area to which it relates.

(3) A notice under subsection (2)(d) must—

(a) describe the proposed scheme, and

(b) state where copies of the proposed scheme and the documents mentioned in subsection (2)(a) to (c) may be inspected.

(4) After giving notice under subsection (2)(d), the authority or authorities must consult—

(a) all persons operating local services in the area or areas to which the proposed scheme relates,

(b) all other persons holding a PSV operator's licence or a community bus permit who would, in the opinion of the authority or authorities, be affected by the proposed scheme,

(c) such persons as appear to the authority or authorities to represent employees of persons falling within paragraph (a),

(d) such organisations appearing to the authority or authorities to be representative of users of local services as they think fit,

(e) any other relevant local authority any part of whose area would, in the opinion of the authority or authorities, be affected by the proposed scheme,

(f) a traffic commissioner,

(g) the chief officer of police for each police area covering the whole or part of an area to which the proposed scheme relates,

(h) the Passengers' Council, and

(i) the Competition and Markets Authority.

(5) In subsection (4)(e) "relevant local authority" means—

(a) a local transport authority,

(b) a district council,

(c) a National Park authority,

(d) the Broads Authority,

(e) a London transport authority, or

(f) a council in Scotland.

(6) The authority or authorities may modify the proposed scheme after consulting those persons and organisations.

123F Consultation document

(1) A consultation document under section 123E(2)(a) relating to a proposed franchising scheme must include—

(a) a description of the area to which the proposed scheme relates,

(b) a description of areas within that area for which different provision is proposed to be made, if such provision is proposed to be included in the proposed scheme,

(c) a description of the local services that are proposed to be provided under local service contracts,

(d) a description of the local services that are proposed to be excepted from regulation arising because of the proposed scheme,

(e) the date on which the scheme is proposed to be made,

(f) the date or dates by which it is proposed that local service contracts first be entered into,

(g) the period or periods it is proposed will expire between the making of local service contracts and the provision of local services under such contracts,

(h) a description of the authority's or authorities' proposed plans for consulting in order to seek views on how well the scheme is working,

(i) a statement about how, in conducting the procurement process for the provision of local services, the authority or authorities propose to facilitate the involvement of small and medium-sized operators in the provision of local services, and

(j) the date by which responses to the consultation must be received.

(2) The consultation document must also include a summary of the assessment prepared under section 123B in relation to the proposed scheme.

123G Response to consultation

(1) A franchising authority or authorities that conduct a consultation under section 123E must publish a report setting out—

(a) the authority's or authorities' response to the consultation;

(b) the authority's or authorities' decision on whether to make a franchising scheme covering the whole or any part of their area or combined area.

(2) The authority or authorities must give notice of the report to a traffic commissioner.

(3) If the authority or authorities decide to make a franchising scheme, the report must set out how, in conducting the procurement process for the provision of local services, the authority or authorities will facilitate the involvement of small and medium-sized operators in the provision of local services.

(4) If a franchising authority are a mayoral combined authority, the function of deciding whether to make a proposed franchising scheme is a function of the combined authority exercisable only by the mayor acting on behalf of the combined authority (including in a case where the decision is to make a scheme jointly with one or more other franchising authorities).

123H Making and publication of scheme

(1) If the authority or authorities publishing a report under section 123G have decided to make a franchising scheme covering the whole or any part of their area or combined area, they must make the scheme, and publish it, at the same time as the report under section 123G.

(2) The scheme must specify—

(a) the area to which the scheme relates,

(b) the local services intended to be provided under local service contracts,

(c) the date on which local service contracts relating to local services may first be entered into (subject to subsection (3)(b)), and

(d) the minimum period that is to expire between the making of a local service contract and the provision of a local service under the contract (subject to subsection (3)(c)).

(3) The scheme may specify—

(a) areas within the area to which the scheme relates ("scheme sub-areas"),

(b) for each scheme sub-area, the date on which a local service contract to provide a local service in that scheme sub-area may first be entered into, and

(c) for each scheme sub-area, the minimum period that is to expire between the making of a local service contract to provide such a service and the provision of such a service under the contract.

(4) A scheme may not specify under subsection (2)(d) or (3)(c) a period of less than six months.

(5) Subject to regulations under section 123U, the scheme may except from regulation arising because of the scheme—

(a) local services specified in the scheme, and

(b) local services of a class specified in the scheme.

(6) If the franchising scheme relates to an area to which a relevant scheme or plan also relates, the franchising scheme must include—

(a) in a case where the relevant scheme or plan relates only to the area to which the franchising scheme relates or a part of that area, provision revoking the relevant scheme or plan, or

(b) in any other case, provision varying the relevant scheme or plan so that it ceases to relate to any part of the area to which the franchising scheme relates.

(7) A franchising scheme may not otherwise vary a relevant scheme or plan.

(8) In subsections (6) and (7)—

"relevant plan" means an enhanced partnership plan, and

"relevant scheme" means an advanced quality partnership scheme or an enhanced partnership scheme.

(9) If provision is made under subsection (6)(b) to vary an enhanced partnership plan or scheme so that it ceases to relate to an area, the local transport authority or authorities to whose area or combined area the plan or, in the case of a scheme, the related plan continues to relate may vary the plan or, as the case may be, the scheme in such manner as they consider appropriate in consequence of the provision made under subsection (6)(b).

(10) Section 138K(3) applies, and section 138K(4), (5) and (8) do not apply, to a variation under subsection (9).

123I Postponement of local service contracts

(1) If it appears to the authority or authorities that have made a franchising scheme appropriate to do so, they may decide that—

(a) the date specified under section 123H(2)(c), or

(b) a date specified under section 123H(3)(b),

is to be postponed (or further postponed).

(2) Before making such a decision they must (if possible) consult—

(a) persons operating local services who would, in their opinion, be affected by the decision;

(b) other persons whom, in their opinion, it would be appropriate to consult.

(3) Within a period of 14 days beginning with the date on which any such decision is made they must give notice of the decision—

(a) in such manner as they consider appropriate for drawing it to the attention of persons in the area to which it relates,

(b) to all persons operating local services who would, in their opinion, be affected by the decision, and

(c) to a traffic commissioner.

(4) The notice must include a statement of the reasons for making the decision.

123J Effect of local service contracts: registration requirements and provision of services

(1) Where a franchising scheme has been made, subsections (2) and (3) apply as soon as the effective time of any local service contract to which the franchising scheme relates is reached, subject to subsection (4).

(2) Sections 6 to 9 of the Transport Act 1985 (registration of local services) do not have effect in relation to the area to which the franchising scheme relates.

(3) No local service may be provided in the area to which the franchising scheme relates (if there is a stopping place for the service in that area) unless—

(a) it is provided under a local service contract,

(b) it is an interim service (see section 123O), or

(c) it is provided under a service permit (see section 123P).

(4) If the scheme provides for scheme sub-areas, subsections (2) and (3) apply in relation to each scheme sub-area as soon as the effective time of any local service contract for the provision of a local service in that scheme sub-area is reached, as if references in subsections (2) and (3) to the area to which the scheme relates were references to the scheme sub-area.

(5) Subsections (2) and (3) do not apply in relation to—

(a) a local service which is excepted from regulation arising because of the proposed scheme by any provision of the scheme that is made under section 123H(5), or

(b) the use of a vehicle under a permit granted under section 22 of the Transport Act 1985.

(6) If it appears to a franchising authority that—

(a) a person is operating or has operated a local service in contravention of subsection (3), and

(b) in operating that local service, the person is failing or has failed to take all reasonable precautions and to exercise all due diligence to avoid contravening subsection (3),

the authority must inform a traffic commissioner.

(7) The effective time, in relation to a local service contract, is the beginning of the day on which a local service may first be provided under the contract (see sections 123K(4) and 123L).

123K Local service contracts

(1) If a franchising scheme covers the whole or part of the combined area of two or more franchising authorities, a local service contract for a local service specified in the scheme is to be entered by the authorities acting jointly.

(2) A franchising authority or authorities may only enter into a local service contract with a person who is the holder of either—

(a) a PSV operator's licence, or

(b) a community bus permit.

(3) But subsection (2)(a) does not include a licence to which a condition is attached under section 26 of the Transport Act 1985 (power of traffic commissioner to attach conditions to licences) prohibiting the holder from using vehicles under the licence to provide local services of all descriptions or of any description to which the condition relates.

(4) A person may not provide a local service under a local service contract until—

(a) the expiry of the period that, under the scheme, must expire between the making of the contract and the provision of the local service under the contract (see section 123H(2)(d) and (3)(c)), or

(b) such later time as may be specified in the contract.

(5) Subsection (4) is subject to section 123L.

(6) If—

(a) a franchising authority or authorities enter into a local service contract, and

(b) the contract is—

(i) the first contract for the provision of a local service specified in the scheme that is entered into, or

(ii) for any scheme sub-area, the first contract for the provision of a local service specified in relation to that scheme sub-area that is entered into,

they must give notice of the contract to a traffic commissioner.

(7) A notice under subsection (6) must be given within a period of 14 days beginning with the date on which the local service contract in question is entered into.

123L Exceptions to section 123K

(1) A local service contract may specify as the time when a local service may first be provided under the contract a time before the expiry of such period as is described in section 123K(4)(a), and that service may be provided from that time, if the authority or authorities determine that action is urgently required for the purpose of—

(a) maintaining an existing service,

(b) securing the provision of a service in place of a service which has ceased to operate, or

(c) securing the provision of a service to meet any public transport requirement which has arisen unexpectedly and ought in the opinion of the authority to be met without delay.

(2) A determination under subsection (1) must be made at or before the time that the authority or authorities enter into the contract.

123M Variation of scheme

(1) The franchising authority or authorities operating a franchising scheme may vary, or acting jointly may vary, the scheme.

(2) If the authority or authorities decide to vary a franchising scheme, the authority or authorities must—

(a) publish a notice of the decision, and

(b) give notice of the decision to a traffic commissioner.

(3) The notice of the decision must state the date on which the variations of the scheme are to have effect.

(4) The date must fall after a period of six months beginning with the date on which notice of the decision is published.

(5) The notice must be published, and notice must be given to a traffic commissioner, within a period of 14 days beginning with the date on which the decision was made.

(6) If a franchising authority are a mayoral combined authority, the function of deciding whether to make a proposed variation is a function of the combined authority exercisable only by the mayor acting on behalf of the combined authority (including in a case where the decision is to act jointly to vary a scheme).

(7) The references in subsections (1) to (6) to the franchising authority or authorities in relation to a franchising scheme include a reference to a franchising authority who are not operating the scheme but would do so under a proposed variation.

(8) The variation of a franchising scheme is subject to the same procedure as the making of a franchising scheme, except that—

(a) the procedure may be modified or excluded in its application to the variation of a scheme by regulations under section 123U,

(b) sections 123B, 123C, 123D and 123F(2) do not apply, and

(c) section 123G(3) does not apply.

(9) If the variation of a franchising scheme would involve adding an area to the area to which the scheme relates, subsection (8) has effect in relation to the variation but without subsection (8)(b).

123N Revocation of scheme

(1) The franchising authority or authorities operating a franchising scheme may revoke, or acting jointly may revoke, the franchising scheme.

(2) The authority or authorities may revoke the scheme only if they are satisfied that—

(a) local services in the area to which the scheme relates are likely to be better if the scheme did not apply,

(b) the continued operation of the scheme is likely to cause financial difficulties for the authority or any of the authorities, or

(c) the burdens of continuing with the scheme are likely to outweigh the benefits of doing so.

(3) If the authority or authorities decide to revoke a franchising scheme, the authority or authorities must—

(a) publish a notice of the decision, and

(b) give notice of the decision to a traffic commissioner.

(4) The notice of the decision must state the date on which the revocation is to have effect.

(5) The date of revocation must fall after a period of six months beginning with the date on which notice of the decision is published.

(6) The notice must be published, and notice must be given to a traffic commissioner, within a period of 14 days beginning with the date on which the decision was made.

(7) If a franchising authority are a mayoral combined authority, the function of deciding whether to make a proposed revocation is a function of the combined authority exercisable only by the mayor acting on behalf of the combined authority (including in a case where the decision is to act jointly to revoke a scheme).

(8) The revocation of a franchising scheme is subject to the same procedure as the making of a franchising scheme, except that—

(a) the procedure may be modified or excluded in its application to the revocation of a scheme by regulations under section 123U, and

(b) section 123G(3) does not apply.

123O Interim services and replacement services

(1) This section applies if—

(a) a franchising authority or authorities have entered into a local service contract with another person ("the operator") about providing a local service ("the original service") for a period, and

(b) the operator fails to provide the original service or ceases to provide the original service before the end of the period.

(2) The authority, or any one of the authorities, may provide a local service (an "interim service") in the place of the original service or a part of it.

(3) Subsection (2) has effect notwithstanding any prohibition, restriction or limitation on the power of the authority to provide local services contained in any other enactment, apart from the restriction in section 22 of the Bus Services Act 2017.

(4) A franchising authority providing an interim service must have a PSV operator's licence to which no condition is attached under section 26 of the Transport Act 1985 (power of traffic commissioner to attach conditions to licence) prohibiting the authority from using vehicles under the licence to provide services of that description.

(5) A franchising authority may not provide an interim service after the end of the period of six months beginning with the day on which the authority begins to provide the service, subject to subsection (7).

(6) If—

(a) an interim service is provided, and

(b) the authority or authorities decide to enter into a local service contract with another person for the provision of a local service (a "replacement service") that would replace the original service or a part of it,

section 123K(4) does not apply in relation to the provision of the replacement service.

(7) If the authority or authorities enter into a local service contract for the provision of a replacement service, the authority or the authority providing the interim service may continue to provide it until the replacement service begins to be provided.

(8) An interim service or replacement service need not be identical to the original service, or the part of the original service, that is replaced by the interim service or the replacement service (and such a change is not to be regarded as a variation of the scheme for the purposes of section 123M).

(9) In this section "enactment" includes an enactment comprised in subordinate legislation (within the meaning of the Interpretation Act 1978).

123P Service permits

(1) This section applies where a franchising scheme covers the whole or part of the area or combined area of a franchising authority or authorities.

(2) The authority or authorities, acting jointly, may grant a permit (a "service permit") authorising a person to provide a local service in the area to which the scheme relates.

123Q Application for service permit

(1) An application for a service permit authorising a person to provide a particular local service in an area to which a franchising scheme relates must be made in such manner as the authority or authorities operating the scheme may determine.

(2) An application must be accompanied by such information as the authority or authorities operating the scheme may specify.

(3) If the authority or authorities so require, an application for a service permit must be accompanied by a fee for processing the application of an amount that is determined in accordance with regulations made by the Secretary of State.

(4) Regulations under subsection (3) may specify the maximum amount of the fee.

(5) The authority or authorities must grant the service permit applied for if they are satisfied that—

(a) the proposed service will benefit persons making journeys on local services in the area to which the scheme relates, and

(b) the proposed service will not have an adverse effect on any local service that is provided under a local service contract in the area to which the scheme relates.

(6) The authority or authorities may not grant the service permit applied for if they are not satisfied as to the matters in subsection (5)(a) and (b).

(7) If the authority or authorities do not grant a service permit, they must give notice of their reasons to the applicant within a period of ten days beginning with the date on which they decide not to grant the service permit.

123R Conditions

(1) A franchising authority or authorities may publish a notice specifying the conditions, or descriptions of conditions, that they may attach to a service permit.

(2) A franchising authority or authorities may—

(a) withdraw a notice under subsection (1), and

(b) if an earlier notice under subsection (1) is withdrawn, publish another notice under subsection (1).

(3) A franchising authority or authorities may only specify in a notice under subsection (1) conditions that are specified, or are of a description specified, in regulations made by the Secretary of State.

(4) Regulations under subsection (3) may in particular provide for conditions requiring holders of service permits to participate in ticketing arrangements.

(5) Before the authority or authorities publish a notice under subsection (1) (or withdraw such a notice), they must consult—

(a) persons operating local services in the area to which the scheme relates, and

(b) other persons whom, in their opinion, it would be appropriate to consult.

(6) If a notice under subsection (1) is published, the franchising authority or authorities may attach to—

(a) a service permit granted by them after the notice is published, or

(b) a service permit already granted by them,

conditions, or conditions of a description, specified in the notice.

(7) If a notice under subsection (1) is withdrawn, conditions attached to service permits granted by the franchising authority or authorities before it was withdrawn cease to have effect (subject to being attached again under subsection (6)(b)).

(8) If the authority or authorities grant a service permit with conditions, they must give notice of their reasons for doing so to the applicant within a period of 14 days beginning with the date on which they grant the service permit with those conditions.

(9) If the authority or authorities attach conditions to a service permit after it is granted, they must give notice of their reasons for doing so to the holder of the service permit within a period of 14 days beginning with the date on which they attach those conditions.

123S Revocation and suspension

(1) A franchising authority or authorities may revoke or suspend a service permit granted by them.

(2) The grounds on which a franchising authority or authorities may revoke or suspend a service permit are—

- (a) that a matter in section 123Q(5)(a) or (b) is not satisfied as regards the service to which the service permit relates,
- (b) that the holder of the service permit has failed to comply with a condition attached to the service permit, and
- (c) that the public would be endangered if the service continued to operate.

(3) The Secretary of State may by regulations make provision about the period of notice that must expire before a revocation or suspension takes effect.

(4) The regulations may, in particular, enable a franchising authority or authorities to revoke or suspend a service permit with immediate effect if the permit is revoked or suspended on the ground mentioned in subsection (2)(c).

(5) A service permit is of no effect during a period of suspension.

123T Appeals

(1) A person whose application for a service permit is refused may appeal against the refusal.

(2) A person who is granted a service permit with conditions may appeal against the attaching of the conditions or any of them.

(3) A person to whose service permit conditions are attached after the service permit is granted may appeal against the attaching of the conditions or any of them.

(4) A person whose service permit is revoked or suspended may appeal against the revocation or suspension.

(5) An appeal under subsection (1), (2), (3) or (4) is to be made to a traffic commissioner.

(6) On an appeal under subsection (1), (2), (3) or (4), a traffic commissioner may—

- (a) uphold the decision,
- (b) quash the decision, or
- (c) substitute a decision for the decision made.

(7) The Secretary of State may by regulations make provision about appeals under this section including, in particular, provision—

(a) as to the time within which an appeal to a traffic commissioner must be brought,

(b) enabling a traffic commissioner to hold a hearing,

(c) requiring a traffic commissioner to hold a hearing if requested by the appellant,

(d) as to the time within which a hearing must be held, and

(e) as to the time within which an appeal must be determined.

(8) A person may appeal to the Upper Tribunal against a decision of a traffic commissioner under subsection (6).

(9) For the purposes of section 13(2) of the Tribunals, Courts and Enforcement Act 2007 (appeals to Court of Appeal etc against decisions of the Upper Tribunal) the following persons are to be treated as parties to a case—

(a) the person who appealed under subsection (1), (2), (3) or (4),

(b) the franchising authority or authorities whose decision was appealed, and

(c) a traffic commissioner.

123U Regulations about schemes

(1) The Secretary of State may by regulations make further provision with respect to—

(a) the procedure to be followed when making, varying or revoking franchising schemes,

(b) the local services or classes of local services which are to be, or may be, excepted from regulation arising because of the scheme, and

(c) such other incidental matters in connection with franchising schemes as the Secretary of State thinks fit.

(2) The regulations may in particular make provision with respect to—

(a) giving notice of proposed schemes or the proposed variation or revocation of schemes,

(b) modifications of such proposals,

(c) the form of schemes or variations, and

(d) giving notice of schemes which have been made or of the variation or revocation of schemes.

(3) The Secretary of State may by regulations make further provision with respect to service permits.

(4) The Secretary of State may also make regulations modifying or excluding the application of provisions of this Part, so far as relating to franchising schemes, in cases where a franchising authority, or two or more franchising authorities acting jointly—

(a) propose or decide to vary or revoke a scheme under section 123M or 123N, or

(b) having varied a scheme under section 123M, propose or decide to postpone a date on which a local service contract to provide a local service specified in the scheme may first be entered into.

123V Transitional provision about schemes

(1) The Secretary of State may by regulations make such transitional provision as the Secretary of State considers appropriate in connection with—

(a) the making of franchising schemes,

(b) the application of section 123J in relation to an area (effect of local service contracts: sections 6 to 9 of the Transport Act 1985 and provision of services),

(c) the variation of franchising schemes, and

(d) the revocation of franchising schemes.

(2) The regulations may in particular provide that in prescribed circumstances—

(a) any provision of sections 6 to 9 of the Transport Act 1985 (registration of local services), or of sections 89 to 92 of that Act (obligation to invite tenders etc), which would otherwise have effect is not to have effect or is to have effect with such modifications as may be prescribed, or

(b) any such provision which would not otherwise have effect is to have effect or is to have effect with such modifications as may be prescribed,

in relation to the whole or any part of the area to which the scheme relates.

(3) Regulations made by virtue of subsection (2) may in particular provide for the period in section 6(8)(a) of the Transport Act 1985 to be, for applications to vary or cancel the registration of services that have one or more stopping places in the area to which a franchising scheme relates, the period specified in a notice issued by the authority or authorities that made the franchising scheme.

(4) The regulations may impose requirements in relation to notices issued as mentioned in subsection (3) that include (but are not limited to) requirements—

(a) as to the time when the notice may be issued,

(b) as to the publication of the notice,

(c) as to sending a copy of the notice to a traffic commissioner, and

(d) as to the period, not exceeding 112 days, that may be specified in the notice.

(5) Regulations made by virtue of subsection (2) may in particular provide for cases where local services continue to be provided in an area under local service contracts after a franchising scheme—

(a) is revoked, or

(b) is varied so as no longer to relate to that area.

(6) The regulations may—

(a) prohibit the registration of a service, or a variation of the registration of a service, under section 6 of the Transport Act 1985 so far as the service, or the service as varied, would be provided in that area, except in a case where the service, or the service as varied, would be a service that, under the scheme as it had effect before it was revoked or varied, could have been provided in that area under a local service contract, and

(b) require a traffic commissioner to register a service on an application by a person who, immediately before the scheme was revoked or varied, provided the same service under a service permit.

(7) Any regulations made by virtue of subsection (1)(a) are not to have effect in the case of any franchising scheme as respects any time before the making of the scheme.

123W Guidance about schemes

(1) The Secretary of State may issue guidance concerning the exercise by franchising authorities of their functions under this Part in relation to franchising schemes.

(2) Franchising authorities must have regard to any such guidance.

123X Local service contracts: application of TUPE

(1) Subsection (3) applies to a situation in which—

(a) at the effective time of a local service contract, local services cease to be provided by a person (the "former operator") in—

(i) the area to which the relevant franchising scheme relates, or

(ii) in the case of a franchising scheme which provides for scheme sub-areas, the relevant scheme sub-area,

in accordance with section 123J(3), and

(b) at the same time, a person (the "new operator") begins to provide local services in that area under that local service contract.

(2) Subsection (3) also applies to a situation in which—

(a) local services which, at the effective time of a local service contract, a person (the "former operator") would be required by section 123J(3) to cease providing in—

(i) the area mentioned in subsection (1)(a)(i), or

(ii) the area mentioned in subsection (1)(a)(ii) (as the case may be),

cease to be provided by the former operator before the effective time of that local service contract, and

(b) at the same time as those local services cease to be provided by the former operator, a person (the "new operator") begins to provide local services in that area under an agreement which the authority or authorities operating the relevant franchising scheme entered into by reason of the cessation of the local services referred to in paragraph (a).

(3) Any situation to which this subsection applies is to be treated as a relevant transfer for the purposes of the Transfer of Undertakings (Protection of Employment) Regulations 2006 ("TUPE") (whether or not TUPE would apply apart from this subsection).

(4) For the purposes of TUPE, the organised grouping of employees that is subject to the relevant transfer consists of those employees of the former operator whose employment is principally connected with the provision of the local services referred to in subsection (1)(a) or (as the case may be) the local services referred to in subsection (2)(a).

(5) Any situation which by virtue of this section is treated as a relevant transfer for the purposes of TUPE is also to be treated as a relevant transfer within the meaning of TUPE for the purposes of—

(a) sections 257 and 258 of the Pensions Act 2004, and

(b) any regulations made under section 258 of that Act.

(6) The Secretary of State may make regulations supplementing the provision made by this section.

(7) The provision that may be made by regulations under subsection (6) includes—

(a) provision for determining, for the purposes of subsection (4), whether a person's employment is principally connected with the provision of any particular local services (including provision for or in connection with the appointment of a person to make such determination);

(b) provision for determining, in the case of any particular organised grouping of employees, the particular new operator who is to be the transferee for the purposes of TUPE (including provision for or in connection with the appointment of a person to make such determination);

(c) provision requiring any person operating local services in the area to which a franchising scheme relates to provide the authority or authorities operating the scheme with such information as may be prescribed, at such time as may be prescribed, about such of that person's employees as would fall within subsection (4) if the person ceased to provide those services in the circumstances described in subsection (1)(a);

(d) provision requiring the authority or authorities operating a franchising scheme to provide all persons operating local services in the area to which the scheme relates with such information as may be prescribed, at such time as may be prescribed, so as to enable such persons to comply with any requirement imposed by virtue of paragraph (c) of this subsection;

(e) provision requiring the authority or authorities operating a franchising scheme to ensure that any local service contract entered into with a person under the scheme, or any other agreement made with a person for the provision of local services in the area to which the scheme relates, is made on terms—

(i) that require the person, in the event of there being any transferring employees, to secure pension protection for every transferring employee, or every transferring employee of a prescribed description, who as an employee of the former operator had rights to acquire pension benefits, and

(ii) that, so far as relating to the securing of pension protection for a transferring employee, are enforceable by the employee.

(8) For the purposes of this section—

(a) "transferring employee" means an employee of a former operator whose contract of employment becomes, either by virtue of TUPE or by virtue of this section, a contract of employment with a new operator;

(b) "pension protection" is secured for a transferring employee if after the change of employer referred to in paragraph (a)—

(i) the employee has, as an employee of the new operator, rights to acquire pension benefits, and

(ii) those rights are of such description as is prescribed by regulations.

(9) The Secretary of State must exercise the power conferred by this section to make regulations containing provision falling within subsection (7)(e) so as to ensure—

(a) that pension protection is required to be secured for every transferring original employee who, as an employee of the original operator, had rights to acquire pension benefits, and

(b) that the rights to acquire pension benefits which a transferring original employee has as an employee of the new operator by virtue of paragraph (a) are rights which—

(i) are the same as the rights the transferring original employee had as an employee of the original operator, or

(ii) under provision made by regulations, count as being broadly comparable to, or better than, those rights.

(10) For the purposes of subsection (9)—

"transferring original employee" means a transferring employee—

(a) who immediately before the relevant date was employed by a person (the "original operator") providing local services in the area to which the relevant franchising scheme relates, and

(b) whose contract of employment—

(i) was, from that date until the change of employer referred to in subsection (8)(a), a contract of employment with the original operator, or

(ii) on each occasion when the employee was subject to a relevant transfer became, either by virtue of TUPE or by virtue of this section, a contract of employment with a person providing local services in the area referred to in paragraph (a);

"relevant date", in relation to a franchising scheme, means—

(a) the date on which the scheme was made, or

(b) where—

(i) the local services being provided by the original operator were not subject to the scheme when it was made, and

(ii) as a result of the variation of the scheme, those services became subject to the scheme,

the date on which that variation was made;

"relevant transfer" means anything that is, or is to be treated as, a relevant transfer for the purposes of TUPE."

5 Power to obtain information about local services

After section 143 of the Transport Act 2000 insert—

"143A Power to obtain information: franchising schemes

(1) A franchising authority may, in connection with their functions under this Part in relation to franchising schemes, require an operator of local services to provide them with such relevant information about local services operated by the operator in the authority's area, or any part of it, as the operator possesses or controls.

(2) If two or more franchising authorities are exercising functions under this Part in relation to the same franchising scheme or proposed franchising scheme, each of them may, in connection with their functions under this Part in relation to franchising schemes, require an operator of local services to provide them with such relevant information about local services operated by the operator in the authorities' areas, or any part of those areas, as the operator possesses or controls.

(3) For the purposes of this section, information about the local services operated by an operator in an area is relevant information if it is—

(a) information about the total number of journeys undertaken by passengers on the local services operated by the operator in the area;

(b) information about the structure of fares for journeys on those local services;

(c) information about revenue received from those local services, including information about revenue attributable to particular types of fares or derived from journeys undertaken on particular parts of those local services;

(d) information about the total distance covered by vehicles used by the operator in operating those local services;

(e) information about persons employed by the operator in the provision of those local services;

(f) information about journeys that the operator has forecast will be undertaken by passengers on those services and revenue that the operator has forecast will be received from those services;

(g) information of such description as is specified in regulations made by the Secretary of State.

(4) The powers in subsections (1) and (2) may not be used to require an operator to provide information relating to periods that fall more than five years before the date of the demand.

(5) If a franchising authority or authorities require the consent of the Secretary of State under section 123C before preparing an assessment under section 123B, that consent must be given before the authority or any of them may exercise the powers in subsections (1) and (2).

(6) The operator may be required—

(a) to provide the information in any form in which, having regard to the manner in which the information is kept, it is reasonable to expect the operator to provide it, and

(b) to provide the information before the end of such reasonable period as may be specified by the franchising authority.

(7) If it appears to a franchising authority that an operator of a local service has failed to take all reasonable steps to comply with a requirement imposed under this section, the authority must inform a traffic commissioner.

(8) A franchising authority that have obtained information under this section may—

(a) use the information for the purposes of their functions under this Part in relation to franchising schemes, and

(b) supply the information to a person specified in subsection (9) for use in connection with the same franchising scheme or the same proposed franchising scheme.

(9) The persons referred to in subsection (8) are—

(a) a franchising authority;

(b) a person providing services to a franchising authority;

(c) a person carrying out functions under section 123D.

(10) The requirements in sections 123E and 123G about publishing documents do not require a franchising authority to publish information obtained by the authority, or another franchising authority exercising functions under this Part in relation to the same franchising scheme or proposed franchising scheme, under this section if it is information that the authority could refuse to disclose in response to a request under—

(a) the Freedom of Information Act 2000, or

(b) the Environmental Information Regulations 2004 (S.I. 2004/3391) or any regulations replacing those regulations."

6 Further amendments

Schedule 2 contains further amendments relating to franchising schemes.

Advanced ticketing schemes

7 Advanced ticketing schemes

In Part 2 of the Transport Act 2000, after section 134B insert—

"Bus services: advanced ticketing schemes

134C Advanced ticketing schemes

(1) A local transport authority whose area is in England, or two or more such authorities acting jointly, may make a ticketing scheme (an "advanced ticketing scheme") covering the whole or any part of their area, or combined area, if they consider that the proposed scheme—

(a) would be in the interests of the public, and

(b) would contribute to the implementation of their local transport policies.

(2) An advanced ticketing scheme may not be made unless the authority or authorities have complied with the notice and consultation requirements imposed by section 134D.

(3) An advanced ticketing scheme is a scheme under which operators of local services of a class specified in it are required to make and implement arrangements under which persons may purchase, in a single transaction, a ticket (or tickets) of any of the descriptions which may be covered by an advanced ticketing scheme and to which the scheme applies.

(4) The descriptions of tickets which may be covered by an advanced ticketing scheme are—

(a) tickets entitling the holder to make more than one journey on particular local services or on local services of a class specified in the scheme (whether or not operated by the same person),

(b) tickets entitling the holder to make a particular journey on two or more local services (whether or not operated by the same person),

(c) where a particular journey could be made on local services provided by any of two or more operators, tickets entitling the holder to make the journey on whichever service the holder chooses, and

(d) tickets entitling the holder to make a journey, or more than one journey, involving both travel on one or more local services and travel by one or more connecting rail or tram services.

(5) A connecting rail or tram service, in relation to an advanced ticketing scheme, is a service for the carriage of passengers by railway or by tramway (or by both) which runs between—

(a) a station or stopping place at or in the vicinity of which local services stop and which serves any part of the area to which the ticketing scheme relates, and

(b) any other place.

(6) The arrangements in an advanced ticketing scheme may make provision for different types of ticket including, in particular—

(a) tickets that are valid for a specified period, and

(b) tickets that are valid only in a specified area.

(7) The arrangements in an advanced ticketing scheme may include—

(a) provision about enabling tickets to be purchased or fares to be paid in particular ways,

(b) provision about the persons from whom tickets may be purchased or to whom fares may be paid,

(c) provision about enabling entitlement to travel to be evidenced in particular ways,

(d) provision about providing information about the arrangements to the public,

(e) provision about publicising local services, fares or ticketing arrangements provided or made available by any operator of a local service of a class specified in the scheme, and

(f) provision as to the appearance of tickets.

(8) Different arrangements may be specified in an advanced ticketing scheme for different cases.

(9) In carrying out their functions under this Part in relation to advanced ticketing schemes, local transport authorities whose areas are in England must co-operate with one another.

(10) In carrying out their functions under this Part in relation to making or varying advanced ticketing schemes, local transport authorities must have regard to the desirability, in appropriate cases, of having a ticketing scheme that—
- (a) facilitates journeys between the area to which the ticketing scheme applies and adjoining areas of England, or
- (b) facilitates the adoption of similar ticketing arrangements in adjoining areas of England.

(11) In considering whether to make or vary an advanced ticketing scheme under this section, a local transport authority must have regard to the desirability, in appropriate cases, of making a scheme jointly with another authority.

134D Notice and consultation requirements

(1) If a local transport authority for an area in England, or two or more such authorities, propose to make an advanced ticketing scheme under section 134C, they must give notice of the proposed scheme in such manner as they consider appropriate for bringing it to the attention of persons in the area to which it relates.

(2) The notice must specify the date on which the scheme is proposed to come into operation.

(3) After giving notice of the proposed scheme, the authority or authorities must consult—
- (a) all operators of local services who would, in the opinion of the authority or authorities, be affected by it,
- (b) such organisations appearing to the authority or authorities to be representative of users of local services as they think fit,
- (c) any other relevant local authority any part of whose area would, in the opinion of the authority or authorities, be affected by the proposed scheme,
- (d) the Passengers' Council,
- (e) the Competition and Markets Authority, and
- (f) a traffic commissioner.

(4) For the purpose of subsection (3)(c) the following are relevant local authorities—
- (a) local transport authorities,
- (b) district councils in England,
- (c) National Park authorities,
- (d) the Broads Authority,
- (e) London transport authorities, and
- (f) councils in Scotland.

134E Making of scheme

(1) If, after consulting in accordance with section 134D, the authority or authorities decide that it is appropriate to make the scheme, they may make it as proposed or with modifications.

(2) If the scheme applies to tickets within section 134C(4)(d), it may only be made with the agreement of the operators of the connecting rail or tram services concerned.

(3) The scheme must specify the date on which it is to come into operation, which must not be earlier than three months after the date on which it is made.

(4) Not later than 14 days after the date on which the scheme is made, the authority or authorities must give notice of the making of the scheme—

(a) in such manner as they consider appropriate for bringing it to the attention of persons in the area to which it relates,

(b) to a traffic commissioner,

(c) to all operators of local services or services for the carriage of passengers by railway or by tramway (or by both) who would, in the opinion of the authority or authorities, be affected by it, and

(d) to the Secretary of State if it applies to tickets within section 134C(4)(d).

(5) The notice must set out the terms of the scheme and the date on which it is to come into operation.

(6) The authority or authorities to whose area or combined area the scheme relates may vary or revoke the scheme.

(7) If the proposed variation would result in the scheme relating to all or part of the area of another local transport authority, the reference in subsection (6) to the authority or authorities includes that other authority.

(8) The variation or revocation is subject to the same procedure as the making of the scheme and in the application of that procedure—

(a) a reference in sections 134C(1) to (9) and 134D and subsections (1) to (5) to making a scheme is to be treated as a reference to varying or revoking a scheme,

(b) a reference in those provisions to the proposed scheme is to be treated as a reference to the scheme as proposed to be varied or to the proposed revocation of the scheme, and

(c) a reference in those provisions to the date on which a scheme comes into operation is to be treated as a reference to the date on which the scheme as varied comes into operation or the date on which the scheme comes to an end.

134F Effect of scheme

During any period in which an advanced ticketing scheme is in operation, operators of local services to which the scheme relates must make and implement the arrangements required by the scheme.

134G Guidance

(1) The Secretary of State may issue guidance concerning the exercise by local transport authorities of their functions under this Part in relation to advanced ticketing schemes.

(2) The authorities must have regard to any such guidance in exercising those functions."

8 Further amendments

Schedule 3 contains further amendments relating to advanced ticketing schemes.

Enhanced partnership plans and schemes

9 Enhanced partnership plans and schemes

In Part 2 of the Transport Act 2000, after section 138 insert—

"Bus services: enhanced partnership plans and schemes

138A Enhanced partnership plans and schemes

(1) A local transport authority whose area is in England, or two or more such authorities acting jointly, may make—

(a) an enhanced partnership plan in relation to the whole or part of their area, or combined area, and

(b) one or more enhanced partnership schemes relating to the whole or part of the area to which the plan relates.

(2) A local transport authority or authorities who have made an enhanced partnership plan may make further enhanced partnership schemes relating to the whole or part of the area to which the plan relates.

(3) An enhanced partnership plan is a plan that—

(a) specifies the area and the period to which the plan relates,

(b) sets out an analysis of the local services provided in that area,

(c) sets out policies relating to local services in that area,

(d) sets out objectives as regards the quality and effectiveness of local services provided in that area by reference to that period,

(e) describes how the related enhanced partnership scheme or schemes is or are intended to assist in implementing those policies and achieving those objectives, and

(f) describes the intended effect of the related enhanced partnership scheme or schemes on areas neighbouring the area to which the plan relates.

(4) An enhanced partnership plan must state whether the plan is to be reviewed and, if so—

(a) specify how it is to be reviewed, and

(b) specify the dates by which reviews are to be completed.

(5) An enhanced partnership scheme is a scheme that—

(a) specifies the area to which the scheme relates, and

(b) imposes requirements in relation to local services that have one or more stopping places in that area by specifying them in the scheme (see section 138C).

(6) An enhanced partnership scheme may also—

(a) require the authority or authorities to provide particular facilities in the area to which the scheme relates (see section 138D),

(b) require the authority or authorities to take particular measures in relation to routes in the whole or part of that area that are served, or might be served, by local services (see section 138D), and

(c) include provision about its variation or revocation (see section 138E).

(7) An enhanced partnership scheme must state whether the operation of the scheme is to be reviewed and, if so—

(a) specify how it is to be reviewed, and

(b) specify the dates by which reviews are to be completed.

(8) An enhanced partnership plan must include a description of the authority's or authorities' plans for consulting such organisations appearing to the authority or authorities to be representative of users of local services as they think fit in order to seek their views on how well the plan and any related scheme are working.

(9) An enhanced partnership scheme may not be made unless the authority or authorities are satisfied that the scheme will contribute to the implementation of—

(a) the policies set out in the related enhanced partnership plan, and

(b) their local transport policies.

(10) An enhanced partnership scheme may not be made unless the authority or authorities are satisfied that the scheme will—

(a) bring benefits to persons using local services in the whole or any part of the area to which the scheme relates by improving the quality or effectiveness of those services, or

(b) reduce or limit traffic congestion, noise or air pollution.

(11) An enhanced partnership plan or scheme may not be made unless the authority or authorities have complied with the requirements in—

(a) section 138F (preparation, notice and consultation), and

(b) section 138G(1) to (4) (making of plan and scheme).

(12) An enhanced partnership plan may not be made without also making an enhanced partnership scheme.

(13) In carrying out their functions under this Part in relation to enhanced partnership plans or schemes local transport authorities must co-operate with each other.

(14) Before making an enhanced partnership plan, a local transport authority must have regard to the desirability, in appropriate cases, of making an enhanced

partnership plan and enhanced partnership schemes jointly with one or more other local transport authorities.

138B Further parties to a scheme

(1) Subsection (2) applies if—

(a) the provision of any of the facilities specified in an enhanced partnership scheme, or

(b) the taking of any of the measures specified in such a scheme,

requires the making of a traffic regulation order in respect of a road or other place in a metropolitan district (other than a road for which the Secretary of State is the traffic authority).

(2) Where this subsection applies, the scheme may not be made unless it is made by—

(a) the local transport authority or authorities, and

(b) the metropolitan district council for the district,

acting jointly.

(3) Subsection (4) applies if—

(a) the provision of any of the facilities specified in an enhanced partnership scheme, or

(b) the taking of any of the measures specified in such a scheme,

requires the making of a traffic regulation order in respect of a road for which the Secretary of State is the traffic authority.

(4) Where this subsection applies, the scheme may not be made unless it is made by—

(a) the local transport authority or authorities, and

(b) the Secretary of State,

acting jointly.

(5) Where subsection (2) or (4) applies so that a metropolitan district council or the Secretary of State makes an enhanced partnership scheme, then (subject to section 138N) the references to the authority or authorities in—

(a) sections 138A(6) and (11),

(b) sections 138F to 138J,

(c) section 138K(1) and (3) to (5),

(d) sections 138L and 138M,

(e) section 138O, and

(f) paragraph 27(4) of Schedule 9 to the Road Traffic Regulation Act 1984,

include (as well as the local transport authority or authorities) the metropolitan district council or the Secretary of State.

(6) Subsection (5) is not to be taken as affecting the area indicated by references in the provisions mentioned in that subsection to the authority's or authorities' area or combined area.

138C Requirements in respect of local services

(1) An enhanced partnership scheme may specify under section 138A(5)(b) requirements about the frequency or timing of particular local services or local services of particular descriptions.

(2) A requirement falling within subsection (1) may, in particular, determine the frequency or timing allowed in relation to a local service—

(a) by reference only to that service, or

(b) by reference to that service and other local services, taken together.

(3) An enhanced partnership scheme may specify under section 138A(5)(b) other requirements as to the standard of services to be provided.

(4) The other requirements referred to in subsection (3) include—

(a) requirements which the vehicles being used to provide local services, or particular descriptions of local services, must meet,

(b) requirements about enabling tickets to be purchased or fares to be paid in particular ways,

(c) requirements about enabling entitlement to travel to be evidenced in particular ways,

(d) requirements about providing information to the public about local services or particular descriptions of local services,

(e) requirements as to the publicising of local services, fares or ticketing arrangements or particular descriptions of local services, fares or ticketing arrangements,

(f) requirements as to the appearance of tickets for local services or particular descriptions of local services,

(g) requirements as to the appearance of vehicles being used to provide local services or particular descriptions of local services,

(h) requirements as to the prices of multi-operator tickets,

(i) requirements as to dates upon which operators may change the timing of local services or particular descriptions of local services, and

(j) requirements as to ticketing arrangements.

(5) The requirements that may be specified under subsection (4)(a) include—

(a) requirements about providing information to passengers by placing particular electronic equipment, or electronic equipment of particular descriptions, in vehicles, and

(b) requirements about emissions or types of fuel or power.

(6) The requirements that may be specified under subsection (4)(b) include requirements about the persons from whom tickets may be purchased or to whom fares may be paid.

(7) The requirements that may be specified under subsection (4)(j) include—

(a) requirements to make arrangements for—

(i) travel to, within or through particular areas,

(ii) travel at particular times,

(iii) travel on particular local services or particular descriptions of local services,

(iv) travel on particular journeys or on particular descriptions of journey, or

(v) travel by persons of particular descriptions,

(b) requirements to make arrangements entitling persons to make a journey, or journeys, involving both travel on one or more local services and travel by one or more connecting rail or tram services, and

(c) requirements about the terms and conditions upon which such travel is made available.

(8) A connecting rail or tram service, in relation to an enhanced partnership scheme, is a service for the carriage of passengers by railway or by tramway (or by both) which runs between—

(a) a station or stopping place at or in the vicinity of which local services stop and which serves any part of the area to which the scheme relates, and

(b) any other place.

(9) The requirements that may be specified in an enhanced partnership scheme also include requirements as to operators of local services establishing and operating arrangements that facilitate the operation of the scheme.

(10) A requirement imposed by an enhanced partnership scheme has effect only in relation to so much of a local service as is provided in the area to which the scheme relates.

(11) An enhanced partnership scheme may not impose requirements in relation to the use of vehicles under permits granted under section 22 of the Transport Act 1985.

(12) In this section "multi-operator ticket" means a ticket, or a number of tickets purchased in a single transaction, entitling the holder to make a journey that involves or may involve, or journeys that involve or may involve, the use of local services provided by more than one operator.

138D Facilities and measures

(1) The facilities which may be specified in an enhanced partnership scheme—

(a) must be facilities provided at specific locations along routes served, or proposed to be served, by local services within the area to which the scheme relates, or facilities which are ancillary to such facilities, but

(b) may not be facilities which are required to be provided as a result of section 139 or 140.

(2) The measures which may be specified in an enhanced partnership scheme—

(a) must be measures taken for the purpose of—

(i) increasing the use of local services serving the routes to which the measures relate or ending or reducing a decline in the use of such services, or

(ii) improving the quality of local services serving the routes to which the measures relate, but

(b) may not include the provision of such facilities as are described in subsection (1)(a) or as are required to be provided as a result of section 139 or 140.

(3) The Secretary of State may by regulations make further provision about the measures which may or may not be specified in an enhanced partnership scheme.

138E Provision relating to variation or revocation

(1) An enhanced partnership scheme may specify cases in which the scheme may be varied or revoked in accordance with the scheme.

(2) The scheme may provide for variation or revocation in a particular case to be subject to satisfying such conditions as the scheme specifies.

(3) The cases that may be specified under subsection (1) as regards variation include cases where the variations in question consist only of such descriptions of variation as are specified in the scheme.

(4) The conditions that may be specified under subsection (2) include conditions prohibiting variation or revocation where a number of operators of local services disagree to the variation or revocation.

138F Preparation, notice and consultation

(1) If a local transport authority or authorities propose to make an enhanced partnership plan and scheme, they must—

(a) give notice of their intention to prepare a plan and scheme in such manner as they consider appropriate for bringing it to the attention of persons in their area or combined area,

(b) prepare a plan and scheme for consultation,

(c) give notice of the plan and scheme prepared to the persons who are operators of qualifying local services in the area to which the plan relates on the relevant day, and

(d) give notice of the proposal to make the plan and scheme in such manner as they consider appropriate for bringing it to the attention of persons in their area or combined area.

(2) A notice under subsection (1)(c) must—

(a) contain full details of the plan and scheme prepared,

(b) state the effect of subsection (5), and

(c) state the period within which objections may be made (which may not be less than 28 days).

(3) A notice under subsection (1)(d) must—

(a) contain full details of the plan and scheme proposed, or

(b) state where such details may be inspected.

(4) A local transport authority or authorities proposing to make an enhanced partnership plan and scheme must—

(a) invite operators of qualifying local services in the area to which the plan relates to participate in the preparation of the plan and scheme before starting to prepare them, and

(b) invite any person who becomes an operator of a qualifying local service in the area to which the plan relates while the plan and scheme are being prepared to participate in that preparation (including any person who becomes such an operator because of a change in the area to which the plan relates while the plan is being prepared).

(5) A local transport authority or authorities may not give notice of a proposal under subsection (1)(d) if, within the period for objections stated in the notice under subsection (1)(c)—

(a) a sufficient number of the persons who, on the relevant day, are operators of qualifying local services in the area to which the plan relates object to the plan prepared, or

(b) a sufficient number of the persons who, on the relevant day, are operators of qualifying local services in the area to which the scheme relates object to the scheme prepared.

(6) After giving notice of the proposed plan and scheme under subsection (1)(d), the authority or authorities must consult—

(a) all operators of local services who would, in the opinion of the authority or authorities, be affected by them,

(b) such organisations appearing to the authority or authorities to be representative of users of local services as they think fit,

(c) any other relevant local authority any part of whose area would, in the opinion of the authority or authorities, be affected by them,

(d) a traffic commissioner,

(e) the chief officer of police for each police area covering the whole or part of the area to which the plan relates,

(f) the Passengers' Council,

(g) the Competition and Markets Authority, and

(h) such other persons as the authority or authorities think fit.

(7) For the purpose of subsection (6)(c) the following are relevant local authorities—

(a) local transport authorities,

(b) district councils in England,

(c) National Park authorities,

(d) the Broads Authority,

(e) London transport authorities, and

(f) councils in Scotland.

(8) If a local transport authority or authorities propose to make a scheme or schemes relating to an existing enhanced partnership plan, subsections (1) to (7) have effect as if—

(a) references to a proposed plan and scheme were references to a proposed scheme or schemes, and

(b) subsection (5)(a) were omitted.

(9) If a local transport authority or authorities propose to make two or more schemes at the same time (whether at the same time as making a plan or in relation to an existing plan), subsection (5)(b) has effect as if references to the scheme were references to one of the schemes in question.

(10) The Secretary of State may by regulations—

(a) specify the descriptions of local services that are qualifying local services for the purposes of this section, and

(b) specify what constitutes a sufficient number of persons for the purposes of subsection (5)(a) or (b).

(11) Regulations under subsection (10)(b) may, in particular—

(a) require that a plan or scheme be objected to by such number of persons as, together, provide at least such proportion of the qualifying local services in the area in question as is specified in the regulations, in addition to being at least such proportion of the persons providing those services as is specified in the regulations, and

(b) make provision about determining the proportion of qualifying local services provided by an operator, including provision about the time by reference to which the proportion is to be determined.

(12) In this section "the relevant day", in relation to an enhanced partnership plan or scheme prepared by a local transport authority or authorities under subsection (1)(b), means the day before the authority or authorities send out a notice relating to that plan or scheme in accordance with subsection (1)(c).

138G Making of plans and schemes

(1) If, after complying with section 138F as regards a proposal to make an enhanced partnership plan and scheme, a local authority or authorities consider it appropriate to make the plan and scheme, they may make them as proposed or with modifications.

(2) If the authority or authorities intend to make the plan and scheme with modifications of one or both of them, the authority or authorities must give notice of their intention to make the plan and scheme, with modifications, to the persons who are operators of qualifying local services in the area to which the plan relates on the relevant day.

(3) A notice under subsection (2) must—

(a) contain full details of the plan and scheme,

(b) state the effect of subsection (4), and

(c) state the period within which objections may be made (which may not be less than 28 days).

(4) The authority or authorities may not make the plan and scheme with modifications if, within the period for objections stated in the notice under subsection (2)—

(a) a sufficient number of the persons who, on the relevant day, are operators of qualifying local services in the area to which the plan relates object to the plan, or

(b) a sufficient number of the persons who, on the relevant day, are operators of qualifying local services in the area to which the scheme relates object to the scheme.

(5) Not later than 14 days after the date on which a local transport authority or authorities make an enhanced partnership plan and scheme, the authority or authorities must give notice of the making of the plan and scheme—

(a) in such manner as they consider appropriate for bringing it to the attention of persons in their area or combined area,

(b) to all operators of local services who would, in the opinion of the authority or authorities, be affected by the scheme, and

(c) to a traffic commissioner.

(6) The notice must—

(a) contain full details of the plan and scheme or state where such details may be inspected, and

(b) if the plan or scheme made is a modified version of the plan or scheme that was proposed, state that it is a modified version.

(7) If the proposal of a local transport authority or authorities is to make a scheme or schemes relating to an existing enhanced partnership plan, subsections (1) to (6) have effect as if—

(a) references to a plan and scheme were references to a scheme or schemes, and

(b) subsection (4)(a) were omitted.

(8) If the proposal of a local transport authority or authorities is to make two or more schemes at the same time (whether at the same time as making a plan or in relation to an existing plan), subsection (4)(b) has effect as if references to the scheme were references to one of the schemes in question.

(9) The Secretary of State may by regulations—

(a) specify the descriptions of local services that are qualifying local services for the purposes of this section, and

(b) specify what constitutes a sufficient number of persons for the purposes of subsection (4)(a) or (b).

(10) Regulations under subsection (9)(b) may, in particular—

(a) require that a plan or scheme be objected to by such number of persons as, together, provide at least such proportion of the qualifying local services in the area in question as is specified in the regulations, in addition to being at least such proportion of the persons providing those services as is specified in the regulations, and

(b) make provision about determining the proportion of qualifying local services provided by an operator, including provision about the time by reference to which the proportion is to be determined.

(11) In this section "the relevant day", in relation to a plan or scheme that a local transport authority or authorities intend to make, means the day before the authority or authorities send out notices relating to that plan or scheme in accordance in subsection (2).

138H Content of scheme

(1) If a local transport authority or authorities make a scheme, the scheme must specify—

(a) the requirements imposed under it,

(b) the facilities (if any) to be provided under it by the authority or authorities,

(c) the measures (if any) to be taken under it by the authority or authorities,

(d) the provision (if any) about variation or revocation of the plan or scheme,

(e) the date on which it is to come into operation, and

(f) the period for which it is to remain in operation.

(2) The scheme must also specify—

(a) if a requirement imposed under the scheme is to have effect as from a date after the scheme comes into operation, the date as from which it has effect,

(b) if any facilities are to be provided under the scheme as from a date after the scheme comes into operation, the date as from which they are to be so provided,

(c) if any measures to be taken under the scheme as from a date after the scheme comes into operation, the date as from which they are to be so taken,

(d) if a condition under section 138E is to apply as from a date after the scheme comes into operation, the date as from which it applies, and

(e) if a condition under section 138E is to cease to apply as from a particular date, the date as from which it ceases to apply.

(3) Subject to regulations under section 138P, the scheme may provide that—

(a) local services specified in it, or

(b) local services of a class specified in it,

are to be excluded from the scheme.

138I Postponement of scheme or part of scheme

(1) If it appears to a local transport authority or authorities that have made an enhanced partnership scheme appropriate to do so, they may decide that any of the dates specified in subsection (3) are to be postponed by such period as they think fit.

(2) A date may not be postponed under subsection (1) by a period or periods which in total exceed 12 months.

(3) The dates are—

(a) the date on which the scheme is to come into operation,

(b) the date as from which any particular requirement is to be imposed under the scheme,

(c) the date as from which any particular facilities are to be provided under the scheme,

(d) the date as from which any particular measures are to be taken under the scheme, and

(e) the date as from which any particular condition under section 138E applies.

(4) Before making such a decision they must consult all operators of local services who would, in their opinion, be affected by the scheme.

(5) Not later than 14 days after the date on which any such decision is made, they must give notice of the making of the decision—

(a) in such manner as they consider appropriate for bringing it to the attention of persons in their area or combined area,

(b) to all operators of local services who would, in their opinion, be affected by the scheme, and

(c) to a traffic commissioner.

(6) The notice must include a statement of their reasons for the decision.

138J Effect of plans and schemes

(1) If an enhanced partnership scheme requires a local transport authority or authorities to provide particular facilities, they must—

(a) provide each of the specified facilities not later than the date specified for its provision under the scheme (subject to section 138I), and

(b) continue to provide it throughout the remainder of the period for which the scheme is in operation.

(2) Subsection (1) does not apply in relation to any period during which the authority or authorities are temporarily unable to provide the facilities because of circumstances beyond their control.

(3) Subsection (1) does not apply in the case of the Secretary of State if the Secretary of State is unable to provide the facilities because of the variation or revocation of a traffic regulation order.

(4) If an enhanced partnership scheme made by a local transport authority or authorities requires them to take particular measures, they must—

(a) take each of the specified measures not later than the date specified for taking it under the scheme (subject to section 138I), and

(b) continue to take those measures throughout the remainder of the period for which the scheme is in operation.

(5) Subsection (4) does not apply in relation to any period during which the authority or authorities are temporarily unable to take those measures because of circumstances beyond their control.

(6) Subsection (4) does not apply in the case of the Secretary of State if the Secretary of State is unable to take the measures because of the variation or revocation of a traffic regulation order.

(7) Subsection (8) applies if the enhanced partnership plan or scheme made by a local transport authority or authorities makes provision about—

(a) one or more reviews of the plan, or

(b) one or more reviews of the operation of the scheme.

(8) The authority or authorities must secure that the review or each review—

(a) is carried out in the manner specified in the plan or scheme, and

(b) is completed by the date specified in the plan or scheme as the date for completing that review.

(9) If a requirement applies to a local service, the operator of the service must comply with that requirement.

(10) Subsection (9) does not apply in relation to services which are excluded from the scheme because of any provision of the scheme made in accordance with section 138H(3).

138K Variation

(1) A local transport authority or authorities to whose area or combined area, or part of it, an enhanced partnership plan relates may vary the plan and any related enhanced partnership scheme.

(2) An enhanced partnership plan or scheme may, in particular, be varied by changing the area to which the plan or scheme relates so that—

(a) it includes the whole or a part of the area of another local transport authority, or

(b) it ceases to include any part of the area of a local transport authority.

(3) An enhanced partnership plan or scheme may not be varied unless the authority or authorities have complied with the requirements in—

(a) section 138L (preparation, notice and consultation), and

(b) section 138M(1) to (5) (making the variation).

(4) An enhanced partnership scheme may not be varied unless the authority or authorities are satisfied that the scheme, as varied, will contribute to the implementation of—

(a) the policies set out in the related enhanced partnership plan (or those policies as proposed to be varied, if the scheme and the policies in the plan are being varied at the same time), and

(b) their local transport policies.

(5) An enhanced partnership scheme may not be varied unless the authority or authorities are satisfied that the scheme, as varied, will—

(a) bring benefits to persons using local services in the whole or any part of the area to which the scheme relates by improving the quality or effectiveness of those services, or

(b) reduce or limit traffic congestion, noise or air pollution.

(6) The references in subsections (1) and (3) to (5) and sections 138L and 138M to the local transport authority or authorities—

(a) in relation to the variation of an enhanced partnership plan, or

(b) in relation to the variation of an enhanced partnership scheme, if the scheme is proposed to be varied at the same time as the related enhanced partnership plan is proposed to be varied,

include a reference to a local transport authority to no part of whose area the plan relates but to whose area or part of it the plan would relate under a proposed variation.

(7) Nothing in this section prevents an enhanced partnership scheme being varied, in accordance with the scheme, in such cases as are allowed by the scheme (see section 138E).

(8) Before varying an enhanced partnership plan, a local transport authority must have regard to the desirability, in appropriate cases, of varying a plan so as to

include in the area to which the plan relates any part of the area of one or more other local transport authorities.

138L Variation: preparation, notice and consultation

(1) If a local transport authority or authorities propose to vary an enhanced partnership plan or scheme, they must—

- (a) give notice of their intention to prepare changes to the plan or scheme in such manner as they consider appropriate for bringing it to the attention of persons in their area or combined area,
- (b) prepare the changes,
- (c) give notice of the changes prepared to the persons who are operators of qualifying local services in the area to which the plan (or the plan as proposed to be varied) relates on the relevant day, and
- (d) give notice of the proposal to vary the plan or scheme in such manner as they consider appropriate for bringing it to the attention of persons in their area or combined area.

(2) A notice under subsection (1)(c) must—

- (a) contain full details of the changes prepared,
- (b) state the effect of subsection (5), and
- (c) state the period within which objections may be made (which may not be less than 28 days).

(3) A notice under subsection (1)(d) must—

- (a) contain full details of the changes, or
- (b) state where such details may be inspected.

(4) The authority or authorities must—

- (a) invite operators of qualifying local services to participate in the preparation of the changes before starting to prepare them, and
- (b) invite any person who becomes an operator of a qualifying local service while the changes are being prepared to participate in their preparation.

(5) A local transport authority or authorities may not give notice of a proposal under subsection (1)(d) if, within the period for objections given in the notice under subsection (1)(c)—

- (a) a sufficient number of the persons who are operators of qualifying local services in the area to which the plan relates on the relevant day object to the changes prepared for the plan (if changes to a plan are prepared), or
- (b) a sufficient number of the persons who are operators of qualifying local services in the area to which the scheme relates on the relevant day object to the changes prepared for the scheme (if changes to a scheme are prepared).

(6) After giving notice of the proposal under subsection (1)(d), the authority or authorities must consult the Competition and Markets Authority.

(7) If a local authority or authorities propose to vary two or more enhanced partnership schemes at the same time, subsection (5)(b) has effect as if references to the scheme were references to one of the schemes in question.

(8) The Secretary of State may by regulations—

(a) specify the descriptions of local services that are qualifying local services for the purposes of this section, and

(b) specify what constitutes a sufficient number of persons for the purposes of subsection (5)(a) or (b).

(9) Regulations under subsection (8)(b) may, in particular—

(a) require that changes to a plan or scheme be objected to by such number of persons as, together, provide at least such proportion of the qualifying local services in the area in question as is specified in the regulations, in addition to being at least such proportion of the persons providing those services as is specified in the regulations, and

(b) make provision about determining the proportion of qualifying local services provided by an operator, including provision about the time by reference to which the proportion is to be determined.

(10) In this section "the relevant day", in relation to changes to an enhanced partnership plan or scheme prepared by a local transport authority or authorities under subsection (1)(b), means the day before the authority or authorities send out a notice relating to that plan or scheme in accordance with subsection (1)(c).

138M Variation: making the variation

(1) This section applies if a local transport authority or authorities have complied with the requirements of section 138L as regards a proposal to vary an enhanced partnership plan or scheme.

(2) If the authority or authorities consider it appropriate to vary the plan or scheme, they may vary the plan or scheme as proposed or with modifications.

(3) Before varying the plan or scheme, the authorities must give notice of their intention to vary the plan or scheme, as proposed or with modifications, to persons who were operators of qualifying local services at the qualifying time.

(4) The notice under subsection (3) must—

(a) contain full details of the variation or state where such details may be inspected,

(b) if the variation made is a modified version of the variation that was proposed, state that it is a modified version,

(c) state the effect of subsection (5), and

(d) specify the period within which persons who are operators of qualifying local services at the qualifying time may object to the proposed variation.

(5) The authority or authorities may not vary the plan or scheme (with or without modifications) if a sufficient number of the persons who were operators of qualifying local services at the qualifying time object to the variation.

(6) Not later than 14 days after the date on which the variation of the plan or scheme is made, the authority or authorities must give notice of the variation—

(a) in such manner as they consider appropriate for bringing it to the attention of persons in their area or combined area,

(b) to all operators of local services who would, in the opinion of the authority or authorities, be affected by it, and

(c) to a traffic commissioner.

(7) The notice must—

(a) contain full details of the variation or state where such details may be inspected, and

(b) if the variation made is a modified version of the variation that was proposed, state that it is a modified version.

(8) The Secretary of State may by regulations—

(a) specify the descriptions of local services that are qualifying local services for the purposes of this section,

(b) provide for the determination of the qualifying time for the purposes of this section,

(c) specify the minimum period which may be specified under subsection (4)(d),

(d) specify what constitutes a sufficient number of persons for the purposes of subsection (5), and

(e) specify how a person's objection is to be evidenced.

(9) Regulations under subsection (8)(d) may, in particular—

(a) require that a proposed variation be objected to by such number of persons as, together, provide at least such proportion of the qualifying local services as is specified in the regulations, in addition to being at least such proportion of the persons providing those services as is specified in the regulations, and

(b) make provision about determining the proportion of qualifying local services provided by an operator, including provision about the time by reference to which the proportion is to be determined.

138N Variation: supplementary

(1) The relevant references to the authority or authorities in relation to an enhanced partnership scheme—

(a) include a traffic regulation authority if it has been varied so that it specifies traffic regulation facilities or measures, but

(b) do not include a traffic regulation authority if it has been varied so that it no longer specifies such facilities or measures.

(2) But if (although the scheme does not specify facilities or measures which are traffic regulation facilities or measures in relation to a traffic regulation authority) it would do by reason of a proposed variation, those references to the authority or authorities in relation to an enhanced partnership scheme (apart from the relevant references in section 138J) include that authority.

(3) And if (although the scheme specifies facilities or measures which are traffic regulation facilities or measures in relation to a traffic regulation authority)—

(a) the traffic regulation order, or (where more than one) each of the traffic regulation orders, required to be made by that authority for the provision of those facilities or measures has been revoked, and

(b) the scheme is proposed to be varied (but not so that it specifies other facilities or measures which are traffic regulation facilities or measures in relation to that authority),

the relevant references to the authority or authorities in relation to an enhanced partnership scheme (apart from those in section 138J) do not include that authority.

(4) For the purposes of this section the relevant references are those in—

(a) section 138A(6) and (11),

(b) sections 138F to 138J,

(c) section 138K(1) and (3) to (5),

(d) sections 138L and 138M,

(e) section 138O, and

(f) paragraph 27(4) of Schedule 9 to the Road Traffic Regulation Act 1984.

(5) Subsections (1) and (2) are not to be taken as affecting the area indicated by references in the provisions mentioned in subsection (4) to the authority's or authorities' area or combined area.

(6) For the purposes of this section—

(a) facilities are traffic regulation facilities, in relation to a traffic regulation authority and an enhanced partnership scheme, if that authority was required to be a maker of the scheme because it originally specified those facilities or would have been required to be a maker of it had it done so, and

(b) measures are traffic regulation measures, in relation to a traffic regulation authority and an enhanced partnership scheme, if that authority was required to be a maker of the scheme because it originally specified those measures or would have been required to be a maker of it had it done so.

(7) In this section "traffic regulation authority" means—

(a) a metropolitan district council, or

(b) the Secretary of State.

138O Revocation

(1) A local transport authority or authorities may, if they consider it appropriate to do so—

(a) revoke an enhanced partnership plan that relates to the whole or any part of their area or combined area, and

(b) revoke an enhanced partnership scheme relating to such a plan.

(2) A local transport authority or authority may not—

(a) revoke an enhanced partnership plan without also revoking all enhanced partnership schemes relating to it, or

(b) revoke all enhanced partnership schemes relating to an enhanced partnership plan without also revoking the plan.

(3) A local transport authority or authorities may not revoke an enhanced partnership plan or scheme unless they have complied with subsections (4) to (8).

(4) A local transport authority or authorities must give notice of a proposal to revoke an enhanced partnership plan or scheme in such manner as they consider appropriate for bringing it to the attention of persons in their area or combined area.

(5) After giving notice under subsection (4), the authority or authorities must consult—

(a) operators of qualifying local services,

(b) the Competition and Markets Authority, and

(c) such other persons as the authority or authorities think fit.

(6) If, after consulting those persons, the authority or authorities wish to revoke the plan or scheme, they must give notice of their intention to revoke the plan or scheme to persons who were operators of qualifying local services at the qualifying time.

(7) The notice under subsection (6) must—

(a) state the date on which the plan or scheme is to be revoked,

(b) state the authority's or authorities' reasons for revoking the plan or scheme,

(c) state the effect of subsection (8), and

(d) specify the period within which persons who are operators of qualifying local services at the qualifying time may object to the revocation.

(8) The authority or authorities may not revoke the plan or scheme if a sufficient number of the persons who were operators of qualifying local services at the qualifying time object to the revocation of the plan or (as the case may be) the scheme.

(9) Not later than 14 days after the date on which the plan or scheme is revoked, the authority or authorities must give notice of the revocation—

(a) in such manner as they consider appropriate for bringing it to the attention of persons in their area or combined area,

(b) to all operators of local services who would, in the opinion of the authority or authorities, be affected by the revocation, and

(c) to a traffic commissioner.

(10) Nothing in subsections (3) to (8) prevents an enhanced partnership scheme being revoked, in accordance with the scheme, in such cases as are allowed by the scheme (see section 138E).

(11) The Secretary of State may by regulations—

(a) specify the descriptions of local services that are qualifying local services for the purposes of this section,

(b) provide for the determination of the qualifying time for the purposes of this section,

(c) specify the minimum period which may be specified under subsection (7)(d),

(d) specify what constitutes a sufficient number of persons for the purposes of subsection (8), and

(e) specify how a person's objection is to be evidenced.

(12) Regulations under subsection (11)(d) may, in particular—

(a) require that the revocation of a plan or scheme be disagreed to by such number of persons as, together, provide at least such proportion of the qualifying local services as is specified in the regulations, in addition to being at least such proportion of the persons providing those services as is specified in the regulations, and

(b) make provision about determining the proportion of qualifying local services provided by an operator, including provision about the time by reference to which the proportion is to be determined.

138P Regulations about plans and schemes

(1) The Secretary of State may by regulations make further provision with respect to—

(a) the procedure to be followed when making, varying or revoking enhanced partnership plans or schemes,

(b) the content or operation of schemes which include a requirement falling within section 138C(1),

(c) the local services or classes of local services which must be, or may be, excluded from schemes,

(d) the making of traffic regulation orders in connection with schemes, and

(e) such other incidental matters in connection with schemes as the Secretary of State thinks fit.

(2) The regulations may in particular make provision with respect to—

(a) giving notice of proposed schemes or proposed variations or revocations of enhanced partnership plans or schemes,

(b) objections to such proposals,

(c) modifications of such proposals,

(d) the form of plans, schemes or variations, and

(e) giving notice of plans or schemes which have been made or of the variation or revocation of plans or schemes.

138Q Transitional provision about schemes

(1) The Secretary of State may by regulations make such transitional provision as the Secretary of State considers appropriate in connection with—

(a) the making of enhanced partnership plans and schemes,

(b) the coming into operation of provisions of enhanced partnership plans and schemes,

(c) the variation of enhanced partnership plans and schemes, and

(d) the revocation of enhanced partnership plans and schemes.

(2) The regulations may in particular provide that in prescribed circumstances—

(a) any provision of sections 6 to 9 of the Transport Act 1985 (registration of local services), or of sections 89 to 92 of that Act (obligation to invite tenders for subsidised services etc), which would otherwise have effect is not to have effect or is to have effect with such modifications as may be prescribed, or

(b) any such provision which would not otherwise have effect is to have effect or is to have effect with such modifications as may be prescribed,

in relation to the whole or any part of the area to which the scheme relates.

(3) The regulations may in particular provide for the application of requirements imposed under section 138A(5)(b) to local services that were registered under section 6 of the Transport Act 1985 before the requirements came into force.

(4) Regulations made by virtue of subsection (3) may in particular—

(a) make provision about recording requirements that apply to local services with the registered particulars of those local services;

(b) make provision requiring the local transport authority or authorities that made an enhanced partnership scheme to notify a traffic commissioner of the local services or the descriptions of local services to which each requirement specified in the scheme would apply, subject to such exceptions as may be prescribed;

(c) make provision for the cancellation of the registration of local services that could not be provided in accordance with requirements falling within section 138C(1);

(d) make provision about the determination by the local transport authority or authorities that made an enhanced partnership scheme of what local services may be registered under section 6 of the Transport Act 1985 in place of local services whose registrations are cancelled under paragraph (c), including provision for awarding contracts authorising the provision of local services or local services of particular descriptions;

(e) make provision as to the period during which the registration, or variation of registration, of local services is subject to provision under paragraph (d);

(f) make provision for cancellation under paragraph (c) to be revoked if prescribed conditions are satisfied, including conditions relating to the variation or cancellation under section 6 of the Transport Act 1985 of the registration of one or more of the local services affected;

(g) make provision for the time at which cancellation under paragraph (c) becomes effective to be postponed in prescribed circumstances;

(h) make provision for appeals against—

(i) decisions to record or not to record requirements under paragraph (a);

(ii) decisions to cancel registrations of local services under paragraph (c).

(5) Regulations made by virtue of subsection (4)(h) may in particular include provision about—

(a) to whom an appeal may be made;

(b) how an appeal may be made and dealt with;

(c) further appeals;

(d) who may be parties to an appeal or further appeal.

(6) In this section "registered particulars", in relation to a local service, means the particulars of the service required to be registered under section 6 of the Transport Act 1985.

138R Guidance about plans and schemes

(1) The Secretary of State may issue guidance concerning the carrying out by local transport authorities and metropolitan district councils of their functions under this Part in relation to enhanced partnership plans and schemes.

(2) Those authorities and councils must have regard to any such guidance.

138S Application of TUPE

(1) Subsection (3) applies to a situation in which—

(a) on the coming into force of an awarded contract, one or more local services cease to be provided by a person (the "former operator") in the area to which the relevant enhanced partnership scheme relates because the cancellation of the registration of the service or services under a relevant provision becomes effective, and

(b) at the same time, a person (the "new operator") begins to provide one or more local services in that area by virtue of that awarded contract.

(2) Subsection (3) also applies to a situation in which—

(a) one or more local services which, on the coming into force of an awarded contract, a person (the "former operator") would be required to cease providing in the area mentioned in subsection (1)(a) of this section because the cancellation of the registration of the service or services under a relevant provision would have become effective, cease to be provided by the former operator before the coming into force of that awarded contract, and

(b) at the same time, a person (the "new operator") begins to provide one or more local services in that area under an agreement which the authority or authorities operating the relevant enhanced partnership scheme entered into by reason of the cessation of the local service or services referred to in paragraph (a).

(3) Any situation to which this subsection applies is to be treated as a relevant transfer for the purposes of the Transfer of Undertakings (Protection of Employment) Regulations 2006 ("TUPE") (whether or not TUPE would apply apart from this subsection).

(4) For the purposes of TUPE, the organised grouping of employees that is subject to the relevant transfer consists of those employees of the former operator whose employment is principally connected with the provision of the local services referred to in subsection (1)(a) or (as the case may be) the local services referred to in subsection (2)(a).

(5) Any situation which by virtue of this section is treated as a relevant transfer for the purposes of TUPE is also to be treated as a relevant transfer within the meaning of TUPE for the purposes of—

(a) sections 257 and 258 of the Pensions Act 2004, and

(b) any regulations made under section 258 of that Act.

(6) The Secretary of State may make regulations supplementing the provision made by this section.

(7) The provision that may be made by regulations under subsection (6) includes—

(a) provision for determining, for the purposes of subsection (4), whether a person's employment is principally connected with the provision of any particular local services (including provision for or in connection with the appointment of a person to make such determination);

(b) provision for determining, in the case of any particular organised grouping of employees, the particular new operator who is to be the transferee for the purposes of TUPE (including provision for or in connection with the appointment of a person to make such determination);

(c) provision requiring any person operating local services in the area to which an enhanced partnership scheme relates to provide the authority or authorities operating the scheme with such information as may be prescribed, at such time as may be prescribed, about such of that person's employees as would fall within subsection (4) if the person ceased to provide those services in the circumstances described in subsection (1)(a);

(d) provision requiring the authority or authorities operating an enhanced partnership scheme to provide all persons operating local services in the area to which the scheme relates with such information as may be prescribed, at such time as may be prescribed, so as to enable such persons to comply with any requirement imposed by virtue of paragraph (c) of this subsection;

(e) provision requiring the authority or authorities operating an enhanced partnership scheme to ensure that any awarded contract entered into with a person because of the scheme, or any other agreement made with a person for the provision of local services in the area to which the scheme relates, is made on terms—

(i) that require the person, in the event of there being any transferring employees, to secure pension protection for every transferring employee, or every transferring employee of a prescribed description, who as an employee of the former operator had rights to acquire pension benefits, and

(ii) that, so far as relating to the securing of pension protection for a transferring employee, are enforceable by the employee.

(8) For the purposes of this section—

(a) "transferring employee" means an employee of a former operator whose contract of employment becomes, either by virtue of TUPE or by virtue of this section, a contract of employment with a new operator;

(b) "pension protection" is secured for a transferring employee if after the change of employer referred to in paragraph (a)—

(i) the employee has, as an employee of the new operator, rights to acquire pension benefits, and

(ii) those rights are of such description as is prescribed by regulations.

(9) The Secretary of State must exercise the power conferred by this section to make regulations containing provision falling within subsection (7)(e) so as to ensure—

(a) that pension protection is required to be secured for every transferring original employee who, as an employee of the original operator, had rights to acquire pension benefits, and

(b) that the rights to acquire pension benefits which a transferring original employee has as an employee of the new operator by virtue of paragraph (a) are rights which—

(i) are the same as the rights the transferring original employee had as an employee of the original operator, or

(ii) under provision made by regulations, count as being broadly comparable to, or better than, those rights.

(10) For the purposes of subsection (9)—

"transferring original employee" means a transferring employee—

(a) who immediately before the relevant date was employed by a person (the "original operator") providing local services in the area to which the relevant enhanced partnership scheme relates, and

(b) whose contract of employment—

(i) was, from that date until the change of employer referred to in subsection (8)(a), a contract of employment with the original operator, or

(ii) on each occasion when the employee was subject to a relevant transfer became, either by virtue of TUPE or by virtue of this section, a contract of employment with a person providing local services in the area referred to in paragraph (a);

"relevant date", in relation to an enhanced partnership scheme, means—

(a) the date on which the scheme was made, or

(b) where—

(i) the local services being provided by the original operator were not subject to the scheme when it was made, and

(ii) as a result of the variation of the scheme, those services became subject to the scheme,

the date on which that variation was made;

"relevant transfer" means anything that is, or is to be treated as, a relevant transfer for the purposes of TUPE.

(11) In this section—

"awarded contract" means a contract authorising a person to provide a local service that is awarded in accordance with—

(a) regulations made by virtue of section 6E(6) of the Transport Act 1985 (provision for services to be allocated), or

(b) regulations made by virtue of section 138Q(4)(d);

and an awarded contract is to be regarded as in force when the authority to provide a service has effect;

"relevant provision" means—

(a) section 6E(2) of the Transport Act 1985 (cancellation where incompatibility with a requirement falling within section 138C(1)), or

(b) regulations made by virtue of section 138Q(4)(c)."

10 Information about local services

After section 143A of the Transport Act 2000 (inserted by section 5) insert—

"143B Power to obtain information about local services: enhanced partnership schemes

(1) If a local transport authority in England, or two or more such authorities acting jointly, are preparing an enhanced partnership plan or scheme, the authority or any of the authorities may, in connection with preparing the plan or scheme, require an operator of a local service in their area or combined area to supply relevant information.

(2) A local transport authority in England that are party to an enhanced partnership plan may, in connection with any relevant function, require an operator of a local service in their area, or in the combined area of the authority and any other local transport authority in England that are party to the plan, to supply relevant information.

(3) If an enhanced partnership plan is proposed to be varied so as to include another local transport authority in England, that authority may, in connection with determining whether and how to vary an enhanced partnership plan or scheme, require an operator of a local service in their area, or in the combined area of that authority and any other local transport authority in England that would be party to the plan as it is proposed to be varied, to supply relevant information.

(4) The operator may be required—

(a) to provide the information in any form in which, having regard to the manner in which the information is kept, it is reasonable to expect him to provide it, and

(b) to provide the information before the end of such reasonable period as may be specified by the local transport authority.

(5) If it appears to a local transport authority that an operator of a local service has failed to take all reasonable steps to comply with a request under this section, the authority must inform a traffic commissioner.

(6) A local transport authority that have obtained information under this section in connection with a function relating to an enhanced partnership plan or scheme may—

(a) use the information for the purposes of the function for which it was obtained, and

(b) supply the information to a person specified in subsection (7) for use for those purposes in connection with the same plan or scheme.

(7) The persons referred to in subsection (6) are—

(a) a local transport authority;

(b) the Secretary of State;

(c) a metropolitan district council;

(d) a person providing services to a local transport authority, the Secretary of State or a metropolitan district council.

(8) A public authority must not disclose information supplied to the authority under this section if it is information which the authority may refuse to disclose in response to a request under the Freedom of Information Act 2000 in reliance on a claim that the information is exempt information by virtue of section 40, 41, 42 or 43 of the Freedom of Information Act 2000.

(9) Subsection (8) does not prevent the disclosure of information—

(a) under subsection (6)(b),

(b) in the case of information relating to the affairs of an individual who is alive or a particular business that is being carried on, with the consent of the individual or the person for the time being carrying on the business,

(c) in connection with the investigation of crime or for the purposes of criminal proceedings,

(d) for the purposes of civil proceedings brought by virtue of this Act or the Transport Act 1985,

(e) in order to comply with the order of a court of tribunal, or

(f) in order to comply with a requirement imposed by law.

(10) The prohibition in subsection (8) is to be disregarded for the purposes of section 44 of the Freedom of Information Act 2000.

(11) In this section—

"relevant function" means—

(a) reviewing an enhanced partnership plan or the operation of an enhanced partnership scheme,

(b) determining whether and how to vary an enhanced partnership plan or scheme, or

(c) determining whether to revoke an enhanced partnership plan or scheme;

"relevant information" means information relating to a local service or passengers on a local service which is of a description specified in regulations made by the Secretary of State."

11 Registration of local services

(1) The Transport Act 1985 is amended as follows.

(2) In section 6 (registration of local services), after subsection (2B) insert—

"(2C) Where—

(a) a requirement imposed under section 138A(5)(b) of the Transport Act 2000 (requirements specified in an enhanced partnership scheme) has effect, and

(b) an application to register a service, or to vary the registration of a service, is made in respect of a service to which that requirement would apply if the application were granted,

section 6D has effect with respect to the application."

(3) In section 6, after subsection (2C) (inserted by subsection (2)) insert—

"(2D) Where—

(a) an enhanced partnership scheme under section 138A of the Transport Act 2000 is in operation,

(b) a service is registered, or a registration of a service is varied, under this section, and

(c) a requirement imposed under section 138A(5)(b) of the Transport Act 2000 applies to the service or the service as varied,

the requirement is to be recorded with the particulars of the service required to be registered under this section."

(4) In section 6, in subsection (9) (regulations for carrying section 6 into effect), after paragraph (h) insert—

"(ha) as to the variation or cancellation of the record of a requirement imposed under section 138A(5)(b) of the Transport Act 2000;".

(5) After section 6C (inserted by section 19) insert—

"6D Applications for registration where an enhanced partnership scheme is in operation

(1) This section applies in any case where—

(a) an enhanced partnership scheme under section 138A of the Transport Act 2000 is in operation;

(b) a requirement imposed under section 138A(5)(b) of the Transport Act 2000 has effect;

(c) an application for registration, or for variation of registration, is made under section 6 of this Act in respect of a local service to which that requirement would apply if the application were granted; and

(d) the application is one which would fall to be accepted, apart from this section.

(2) A traffic commissioner must refuse the application if—

(a) the requirement is an operation requirement, and

(b) the traffic commissioner considers that the person who would be the operator of—

(i) the service proposed to be provided, or,

(ii) the service as proposed to be varied,

is unlikely to be able to comply with that requirement as regards that service.

(3) If, where the requirement is a route requirement, the registration, or variation of registration, of the service under section 6 is prevented by regulations under section 6E(6), a traffic commissioner must refuse the application.

(4) In this section—

"operation requirement" means a requirement imposed under section 138A(5)(b) of the Transport Act 2000, other than a route requirement;

"route requirement" means a requirement imposed under section 138A(5)(b) of the Transport Act 2000 that falls within section 138C(1) of that Act."

12 Cancellation of registration etc

(1) The Transport Act 1985 is amended as follows.

(2) In section 6, after subsection (7A) insert—

"(7B) Where an enhanced partnership scheme under section 138A of the Transport Act 2000 is in operation, the registration of a service may also be cancelled under section 6E."

(3) After section 6D (inserted by section 11) insert—

"6E Cancellation and control of registration where enhanced partnership scheme is in operation

(1) This section applies in a case where—

(a) an enhanced partnership scheme under section 138A of the Transport Act 2000 is in operation, and

(b) one or more requirements imposed under section 138A(5)(b) of the Transport Act 2000 by the scheme have effect.

(2) If a traffic commissioner considers that—

(a) an operation requirement imposed by the scheme applies to a service registered under section 6, and

(b) the service is not being provided in accordance with that requirement,

the traffic commissioner may cancel the registration of that service.

(3) If a traffic commissioner considers that—

(a) a route requirement imposed by the scheme applies to a service registered under section 6, and

(b) that service cannot be provided in accordance with that requirement,

the traffic commissioner must cancel the registration of that service.

(4) If a traffic commissioner considers that—

(a) a route requirement imposed by the scheme applies to two or more services registered under section 6, and

(b) those services cannot all be provided in accordance with that requirement,

the traffic commissioner must cancel the registration of those services.

(5) Subject to regulations under this section, a cancellation of the registration of a service under subsection (2), (3) or (4) becomes effective on the expiry of the period beginning with the date on which a traffic commissioner gives notice to the operator of the service of the cancellation of the registration and ending with the date determined in accordance with regulations under this section.

(6) Regulations under this section may make provision controlling the registration, or the variation of registration, under section 6 of local services which would, or would as varied, be subject to a route requirement by reference to which a registration or registrations was or were cancelled under subsection (3) or (4).

(7) Regulations under subsection (6) may, in particular—

(a) provide for the determination of the services that may be registered and the persons who may register such services;

(b) provide for those matters to be determined by the local transport authority or authorities operating the enhanced partnership scheme;

(c) provide for the authority or authorities to award contracts authorising persons to provide local services or local services of particular descriptions;

(d) provide for services not to be registered under section 6, and for variations of registration under section 6 not to be made, in prescribed cases;

(e) make provision as to the period during which the registration, or variation of registration, of local services under section 6 is subject to provision under subsection (6).

(8) Regulations may be made for the purpose of carrying this section into effect and any such regulations may, in particular—

(a) make provision as to the procedure for cancellation under this section, including provision for giving notice of an intention to cancel unless an operator of a local service satisfies prescribed conditions;

(b) make provision for cancellation under subsection (3) or (4) to be revoked if prescribed conditions are satisfied, including conditions relating to the variation or cancellation under section 6 of the registration of one or more of the services affected;

(c) make provision for the time at which cancellation under subsection (3) or (4) becomes effective to be postponed in prescribed circumstances.

(9) In this section—

"local transport authority" has the meaning given in section 108(4) of the Transport Act 2000;

"operation requirement" and "route requirement" have the same meaning as in section 6D."

13 Appeals

After section 6E of the Transport Act 1985 (inserted by section 12) insert—

"6F Enhanced partnership schemes: appeals

(1) A person may appeal to the Upper Tribunal against—

(a) a decision to record a requirement under section 6(2D) (recording of requirements specified in an enhanced partnership scheme) in relation to a service provided by the person,

(b) a refusal under section 6D(2) or (3) of an application made by the person, or

(c) a cancellation under section 6E of the registration of a service provided by the person.

(2) But if the decision, refusal or cancellation was made by a local transport authority by virtue of section 6G—

(a) the appeal as regards that matter is to be made to a traffic commissioner, and

(b) the local transport authority or authorities operating the relevant enhanced partnership scheme under section 138A of the Transport Act 2000 is or are to be parties to the proceedings.

(3) On an appeal under subsection (2), a traffic commissioner may—

(a) uphold the decision,

(b) quash the decision, or

(c) substitute a decision for the decision made.

(4) Regulations may make provision—

(a) as to the time within which, and the manner in which, appeals under subsection (2) may be made, and

(b) as to the procedure to be followed in connection with such appeals.

(5) A decision of a traffic commissioner on an appeal under subsection (2) may be appealed to the Upper Tribunal by—

(a) the person who appealed under subsection (2), or

(b) the local transport authority or authorities operating the relevant enhanced partnership scheme.

(6) A local transport authority or authorities operating an enhanced partnership scheme under section 138A of the Transport Act 2000 may appeal to the Upper Tribunal against—

(a) a decision of a traffic commissioner to register a service that has a stopping place in the area to which the scheme relates, or

(b) a decision of a traffic commissioner not to record a requirement under section 6(2D) in relation to such a service.

(7) For the purposes of section 13(2) of the Tribunals, Courts and Enforcement Act 2007 (appeals to Court of Appeal etc against decisions of the Upper Tribunal) the following persons are to be treated as parties to a case—

(a) the person whose service is in question;

(b) the local transport authority or authorities operating the relevant enhanced partnership scheme; and

(c) a traffic commissioner.

(8) In this section "local transport authority" has the meaning given in section 108(4) of the Transport Act 2000."

14 Traffic commissioner functions

(1) The Transport Act 1985 is amended as follows.

(2) After section 6F (inserted by section 13) insert—

"6G Traffic commissioner functions where an enhanced partnership scheme in operation

(1) This section applies where notice of—

(a) the making of an enhanced partnership scheme under section 138A of the Transport Act 2000, or

(b) the varying of an enhanced partnership scheme,

is given to a traffic commissioner under section 138G(5) or 138M(6) of the Transport Act 2000 by a local transport authority or authorities.

(2) The authority or authorities must also notify the traffic commissioner—

(a) whether or not the scheme, or the scheme as varied, specifies a route requirement, and

(b) in relation to each route requirement specified, whether or not it relates to—

(i) a particular service that only has stopping places in the area to which the scheme relates,

(ii) particular services at least one of which is such a service, or

(iii) a particular description of services which includes or is capable of including such a service.

(3) In a case where the scheme, or the scheme as varied, relates to the whole or part of the combined area of two or more local transport authorities, the notification under subsection (2) must also state which of the authorities is the lead authority.

(4) If the scheme, or the scheme as varied, specifies a route requirement that relates to a particular service that only has stopping places in the area to which the scheme relates, particular services at least one of which is such a service or a particular description of services which includes or is capable of including such a service—

(a) a traffic commissioner must delegate the relevant registration functions as regards services that only have stopping places in that area to the authority or the lead authority (as the case may be), and

(b) the authority or the lead authority (as the case may be) must carry them out.

(5) A delegation under subsection (4) has effect—

(a) when the scheme comes into operation, or

(b) when the variation of the scheme takes effect (as the case may be).

(6) If subsection (4) does not apply, the authority or the lead authority (as the case may be)—

(a) may elect to carry out the relevant registration functions as regards services that only have stopping places in the area to which the scheme relates as from a particular time, and

(b) if that election is made, must notify a traffic commissioner of that election and the time selected.

(7) If notification is given under subsection (6), a traffic commissioner must delegate the relevant registration functions to—

(a) the authority, or

(b) the lead authority (as the case may be);

and the authority or the lead authority (as the case may be) must carry them out.

(8) A delegation under subsection (4) or (7) may come to end only when the scheme in question ceases to operate.

(9) Regulations may be made for the purpose of carrying this section into effect.

(10) In this section—

"local transport authority" has the meaning given in section 108(4) of the Transport Act 2000;

"the relevant registration functions", in relation to an enhanced partnership scheme, means the functions of a traffic commissioner under sections 6, 6D and 6E of this Act so far as relating to—

(a) in the case of functions relating to the variation of registration, services that would be relevant services if varied as proposed, or

(b) in the case of any other function, relevant services;

"relevant service", in relation to an enhanced partnership scheme, means a local service that only has stopping places in the area to which the scheme relates;

"route requirement" has the same meaning as in section 6D."

(3) After section 6G (inserted by subsection (2)) insert—

"6H Fees relating to relevant registration functions

(1) This section applies where the relevant registration functions of a traffic commissioner are carried out by a local transport authority in accordance with section 6G.

(2) The local transport authority may charge fees under this section in respect of—

(a) an application under section 6 of this Act for the registration of a relevant service,

(b) an application under section 6 of this Act for the variation of the registration of a service that, as varied, would be or continue to be a relevant service, and

(c) an application under section 6 of this Act for the cancellation of the registration of a relevant service.

(3) The fees—

(a) are to be determined by or in accordance with regulations,

(b) are to be payable by such persons and at such times as the regulations may provide, and

(c) are to be payable in one sum or in instalments, as provided by the regulations.

(4) If a fee or instalment of a fee due under this section has not been paid, the local transport authority may decline to proceed with an application referred to in subsection (2) to which the fee or instalment relates until the fee or instalment is paid.

(5) Amounts received in respect of fees charged under this section are not payable to the traffic commissioner (and accordingly may be retained by a local transport authority).

(6) Where this section applies, fees may not be charged under section 52 of the 1981 Act (as applied by section 126 of this Act) in respect of an application referred to in subsection (2).

(7) In this section—

"local transport authority" has the meaning given in section 108(4) of the Transport Act 2000;

"relevant service" has the same meaning as in section 6G;

"the relevant registration functions" has the same meaning as in section 6G."

(4) After section 6H (inserted by subsection (3)) insert—

"6I Records of registration etc

(1) This section applies where the relevant registration functions of a traffic commissioner are carried out by a local transport authority in accordance with section 6G.

(2) The local transport authority must keep a record of—

(a) the local services that are registered and the registrations that are varied or cancelled by the authority under section 6;

(b) the requirements imposed under section 138A(5)(b) of the Transport Act 2000 that are recorded by the authority as applying to services registered under section 6;

(c) the local services that are cancelled by the authority under section 6E.

(3) The authority must allow the record to be inspected at all reasonable times by members of the public.

(4) The authority must supply to a traffic commissioner particulars of—

(a) the local services that are registered and the registrations that are varied or cancelled by the authority under section 6;

(b) the requirements imposed under section 138A(5)(b) of the Transport Act 2000 that are recorded by the authority as applying to services registered under section 6;

(c) the local services that are cancelled by the authority under section 6E.

(5) A record kept under this section is admissible in evidence of the matters required under this section to be entered in that record.

(6) A copy of an entry made in such a record in pursuance of this section purporting to be—

(a) signed on behalf of the authority by which the record is kept, and

(b) certified as a true copy,

is evidence of the matters stated in that entry without proof of the signature or authority of the person signing it.

(7) Regulations may be made for the purpose of carrying this section into effect and any such regulations may, in particular, make provision—

(a) as to the form of records under this section and the particulars they must contain;

(b) as to the particulars to be supplied to a traffic commissioner under this section.

(8) In this section—

"local transport authority" has the meaning given in section 108(4) of the Transport Act 2000;

"the relevant registration functions" has the same meaning as in section 6G."

15 Further amendments

Schedule 4 contains further amendments relating to enhanced partnership plans and schemes.

Powers to make traffic regulation orders

16 Powers to make traffic regulation orders

(1) The Road Traffic Regulation Act 1984 is amended as follows.

(2) In section 1 (traffic regulation orders outside Greater London), in subsection (3A), after "facilities" insert "or for the taking of relevant bus scheme measures".

(3) In section 1(3B), before paragraph (a) insert—

"(za) facilities provided pursuant to an advanced quality partnership scheme under Part 2 of the Transport Act 2000;".

(4) In section 1(3B), in paragraph (a), for "Part 2 of the Transport Act 2000" substitute "that Part".

(5) In section 1(3B), after paragraph (a), insert—

"(aa) facilities provided in connection with a franchising scheme under that Part (see section 123A(3)(d) of that Act);".

(6) In section 1(3B), after paragraph (b) insert—

"(c) facilities provided pursuant to an enhanced partnership scheme under that Part."

(7) In section 1, after subsection (3B) insert—

"(3C) In subsection (3A) "relevant bus scheme measures" means—

(a) measures taken pursuant to an advanced quality partnership scheme under Part 2 of the Transport Act 2000;

(b) measures taken pursuant to an enhanced partnership scheme under that Part."

(8) In Schedule 9 (special provisions as to certain orders), in paragraph 27 (variation or revocation of orders under section 1 etc), in sub-paragraph (1), for "and (3)" substitute ", (2A), (3) and (4)".

(9) In paragraph 27 of that Schedule, after sub-paragraph (2) insert—

"(2A) Where an order is required for the provision of facilities or the taking of measures pursuant to an advanced quality partnership scheme made under Part 2 of the Transport Act 2000 by more than one authority—

(a) it may not be varied or revoked by virtue of this paragraph by the Secretary of State unless the Secretary of State has consulted the other authority or authorities who made the scheme, and

(b) it may not be varied or revoked by virtue of this paragraph by any other authority without the consent of that other authority or those other authorities."

(10) In paragraph 27 of that Schedule, after sub-paragraph (3) insert—

"(4) Where an order is required for the provision of facilities or the taking of measures pursuant to an enhanced partnership scheme made under Part 2 of the Transport Act 2000 by more than one authority—

(a) it may not be varied or revoked by virtue of this paragraph by the Secretary of State unless the Secretary of State has consulted the other authority or authorities who made the scheme, and

(b) it may not be varied or revoked by virtue of this paragraph by any other authority without the consent of that other authority or those other authorities."

Information for bus passengers

17 Information for bus passengers

(1) After section 181 of the Equality Act 2010 insert—

"**CHAPTER 2A**

BUS SERVICES

181A Information for bus passengers

(1) The Secretary of State may, for the purpose of facilitating travel by disabled persons, make regulations requiring operators of local services to make available information about a local service to persons travelling on the service.

(2) The regulations may make provision about—

(a) the descriptions of information that are to be made available;

(b) how information is to be made available.

(3) The regulations may, in particular, require an operator of a local service to make available information of a prescribed description about—

(a) the name or other designation of the local service;

(b) the direction of travel;

(c) stopping places;

(d) diversions;

(e) connecting local services.

(4) The regulations may, in particular—

(a) specify when information of a prescribed description is to be made available;

(b) specify how information of a prescribed description is to be made available, including requiring information to be both announced and displayed;

(c) specify standards for the provision of information, including standards based on an announcement being audible or a display being visible to a person of a prescribed description in a prescribed location;

(d) specify forms of communication that are not to be regarded as satisfying a requirement to make information available.

(5) Regulations under this section may make different provision—

(a) as respects different descriptions of vehicle;

(b) as respects the same description of vehicle in different circumstances.

(6) Before making regulations under this section, the Secretary of State must consult—

(a) the Welsh Ministers;

(b) the Scottish Ministers.

181B Exemptions etc

(1) The Secretary of State may by regulations make provision for securing that the provisions of regulations under section 181A do not apply or apply subject to such modifications or exceptions as the regulations may specify to—

(a) public service vehicles of a prescribed description;

(b) operators of a prescribed description;

(c) local services of a prescribed description.

(2) Regulations under subsection (1)(b) may, in particular, make provision by reference to an operator's size.

(3) Regulations under this section may also make provision for securing that the provisions of regulations under section 181A do not apply or apply subject to such modifications or exceptions as the regulations may specify to—

(a) a prescribed public service vehicle;

(b) public service vehicles of a prescribed operator;

(c) a prescribed local service.

(4) Regulations under subsection (1) or (3) may make the provision subject to such restrictions and conditions as are specified in the regulations.

(5) Regulations under subsection (1) or (3) may specify the period for which provisions of those regulations are to have effect.

(6) Regulations under subsection (1) may make different provision for different areas.

(7) Section 207(2) does not require regulations under this section that apply only to—

(a) a prescribed public service vehicle,

(b) public service vehicles of a prescribed operator, or

(c) a prescribed local service,

to be made by statutory instrument; but such regulations are as capable of being amended or revoked as regulations made by statutory instrument.

(8) Before making regulations under this section, the Secretary of State must consult—

(a) the Welsh Ministers;

(b) the Scottish Ministers.

181C Guidance

(1) The Secretary of State must issue guidance about the duties imposed on operators of local services by regulations under section 181A.

(2) The Secretary of State—

(a) must review the guidance issued under subsection (1), at intervals not exceeding five years, and

(b) may revise it.

(3) Before issuing the guidance or revising it in a way which would, in the opinion of the Secretary of State, result in a substantial change to it, the Secretary of State must consult—

(a) the Welsh Ministers,

(b) the Scottish Ministers,

(c) the Passengers' Council,

(d) such organisations representing disabled persons, including the Disabled Persons Transport Advisory Committee and the committee established under section 72 of the Transport (Scotland) Act 2001, as the Secretary of State thinks fit,

(e) such organisations representing operators of local services as the Secretary of State thinks fit, and

(f) such other persons as the Secretary of State thinks fit.

(4) The Secretary of State must arrange for any guidance issued or revised under this section to be published in a way the Secretary of State considers appropriate.

181D Interpretation

(1) In this Chapter—

"local service" has the same meaning as in the Transport Act 1985;

"public service vehicle" means a vehicle that is a public service vehicle for the purposes of the Public Passenger Vehicles Act 1981;

"stopping place" has the same meaning as in the Transport Act 1985.

(2) For the purposes of this Chapter, a local service ("service A") is a connecting local service in relation to another local service ("service B") if service A has a stopping place at, or in the vicinity of, a stopping place of service B.

(3) References in this Chapter to the operator of a passenger transport service of any description are to be construed in accordance with section 137(7) of the Transport Act 1985."

(2) In section 207 of that Act (exercise of power to make orders and regulations), in subsection (5), after "174(4)" insert ", 181A(5), 181B(6)".

(3) In section 208 of that Act (procedure for orders and regulations), in subsection (5) (statutory instruments subject to affirmative procedure), after paragraph (f) insert—

"(fa) regulations under section 181A or 181B (information for bus passengers);".

(4) In section 26 of the Transport Act 1985 (conditions attached to PSV operators' licence), in subsection (1), after paragraph (bb) insert—

"(bc) the operator has failed to comply with a requirement of regulations made under section 181A of the Equality Act 2010;".

(5) In section 155 of the Transport Act 2000 (sanctions), after subsection (1ZD) (inserted by Schedule 4), insert—

"(1ZE) Where a traffic commissioner is satisfied that the operator of a local service has, without reasonable excuse, failed to comply with a requirement of regulations made under section 181A of the Equality Act 2010, the traffic commissioner may make one or more orders under subsection (1A)(a) or (d)."

(6) In section 39 of the Transport (Scotland) Act 2001 (penalties), in subsection (1)—

(a) omit the "or" following paragraph (b);

(b) after paragraph (c) insert "; or

(d) failed to comply with a requirement of regulations made under section 181A of the Equality Act 2010,".

Information about English bus services

18 Power to require provision of information about English bus services

(1) After section 141 of the Transport Act 2000 insert—

"141A Power to require provision of information about English bus services

(1) The Secretary of State may by regulations require—

(a) applicants for the registration of relevant local services, or for the variation or cancellation of any such registration, to provide prescribed information—

(i) in relation to the services, or

(ii) in connection with the application;

(b) operators of registered relevant local services to provide prescribed information in relation to the services;

(c) local transport authorities to provide prescribed information in relation to relevant local services which have one or more stopping places in their areas;

(d) traffic commissioners to provide prescribed information that is held by them in relation to relevant local services.

(2) The information that may be prescribed is such information within subsection (3) as appears to the Secretary of State to be required—

(a) in order to make information about relevant local services available to users or prospective users of those services, or

(b) in order to facilitate the exercise of functions relating to the registration of relevant local services.

(3) The information within this subsection is—

(a) information about routes, stopping places, timetables, fares and tickets,

(b) information about changes or proposed changes to routes, stopping places, timetables, fares and tickets, and

(c) information about the operation of the services.

(4) The information within subsection (3)(c) includes—

(a) live information, that is to say information provided immediately it becomes available about the location of vehicles operating the services and the time at which they stop, or are expected to stop, at stopping places, and

(b) information about the operation of the services in the past.

(5) The regulations may make provision about—

(a) the person to whom the information is to be provided,

(b) the time when it is to be provided, and

(c) the manner and form in which it is to be provided (including, in particular, provision requiring it to be provided electronically).

(6) The provision made under subsection (5)(a) may not require the information to be provided to a person other than—

(a) the Secretary of State;

(b) a local transport authority whose area is in England;

(c) a person prescribed in the regulations, being a person who provides or facilitates the provision of, or is to provide or facilitate the provision of, information about relevant local services to users or prospective users of those services.

(7) The regulations may provide that a reference in the regulations to a standard according to which the information is to be provided is to be construed as a reference to that standard as it has effect from time to time.

(8) The regulations may make provision as to the use and disclosure of the information, including—

(a) provision for the information to be made available free of charge and without restrictions on its use and disclosure, and

(b) provision for information provided in connection with an application for registration, or for the variation or cancellation of a registration, to be provided to a traffic commissioner.

(9) The regulations may make different provision for different areas.

(10) Before making regulations under this section the Secretary of State must consult—

(a) such persons or organisations as appear to the Secretary of State to represent the interests of operators and users of relevant local services,

(b) such persons or organisations as appear to the Secretary of State to represent the interests of local transport authorities whose areas are in England, and

(c) such other persons or organisations as the Secretary of State considers appropriate.

(11) The references to traffic commissioners in subsections (1)(d) and (8)(b) are to be read as including references to any local transport authority carrying out the functions of a traffic commissioner in accordance with section 6G of the Transport Act 1985.

(12) In this section—

(a) "relevant local service" means a local service which has one or more stopping places in the relevant area,

(b) references to registration, in relation to a relevant local service, are to registration under section 6 of the Transport Act 1985,

(c) "prescribed" means prescribed by regulations under this section, and

(d) "relevant area" means England outside Greater London.

(13) Where a local service is or is to be provided both inside and outside the relevant area, any part of the service which is or is to be provided outside the relevant area is to be treated as a separate service for the purposes of subsection (12)(a) if there is any stopping place for that part of the service outside the relevant area."

(2) In section 155(1)(c) of that Act (sanctions), at the end insert "or with regulations under section 141A of this Act".

(3) In section 160 of that Act (regulations and orders under Part 2)—

(a) in subsection (2), after "138F(10), 138G(9)" (inserted by Schedule 4 to this Act) insert "or 141A(1) or";

(b) in subsection (2A) (inserted by Schedule 2 to this Act), after "138F(10), 138G(9)" (inserted by Schedule 4 to this Act) insert "or 141A(1)".

(4) In section 6 of the Transport Act 1985 (registration), at the end of subsection (9)(e) insert "(or, if the applicant is subject to requirements imposed by regulations made by virtue of section 141A(1)(a) of the Transport Act 2000, complies with those requirements)".

Registration of bus services

19 Variation or cancellation of registration: service information

(1) After section 6B of the Transport Act 1985 insert—

"6C Variation or cancellation of registration: service information

(1) Regulations may require the operator of a local service registered under section 6 to provide prescribed information to any local transport authority in England in whose area the service has a stopping place if—

(a) the operator—

(i) has made an application under section 6 to vary or cancel the registration of the service, or

(ii) has notified the local transport authority in accordance with regulations under that section that it proposes to make such an application, and

(b) the authority requests the operator to provide the information.

(2) The information that may be prescribed is information relating to—

(a) the number of passengers using the service, the journeys made by those passengers and the fares paid by them, and

(b) the revenue obtained by operating the service.

(3) Regulations under this section may, in particular—

(a) make provision about the periods of time in respect of which information may be required,

(b) make provision about the time when, and the manner and form in which, information is to be provided,

(c) provide for a traffic commissioner or a body carrying out a traffic commissioner's functions in accordance with section 6G not to accept an application to vary or cancel the service if the operator has failed to comply with the regulations,

(d) make provision about the use and disclosure of information provided under the regulations (including provision about its further disclosure),

(e) make provision as to cases in which section 67 of the 1981 Act does not apply in relation to contraventions of, or failures to comply with, the regulations,

(f) make provision subject to conditions, and

(g) make supplementary, incidental, consequential or transitional provision.

(4) In this section "local transport authority" has the meaning given in section 108(4) of the Transport Act 2000."

(2) In section 155(1) of the Transport Act 2000 (sanctions), after paragraph (aa) insert—

"(ab) failed to comply with a requirement to provide information imposed by virtue of section 6C of that Act,".

20 Rail replacement bus services

(1) In section 6 of the Transport Act 1985 (registration of local services), in subsection (1), after "(1A)" insert "or (1D)".

(2) After subsection (1C) of that section insert—

"(1D) A service falls within this subsection if—

(a) it has one or more stopping places in England, and

(b) it is provided under an agreement entered into, where a railway service has been temporarily interrupted, with the person who usually provides the railway service.

(1E) Where a service is provided both inside and outside England, any part of the service which is provided outside England is to be treated as a separate service for the purposes of subsection (1D) if there is any stopping place for that part of the service outside England."

(3) In section 179 of the Greater London Authority Act 1999 (London local services), for subsection (3) substitute—

"(3) The following are not London local services for the purposes of this Act—

(a) a service provided in pursuance of an agreement with the Secretary of State entered into under section 40 of the Railways Act 2005 (substitution services provided for interrupted or discontinued railway services);

(b) a service provided under an agreement entered into, where a railway service has been temporarily interrupted, with the person who usually provides the railway service."

21 Registration of English local services: fees where functions contracted out

After section 6I of the Transport Act 1985 (inserted by section 14) insert—

"6J Contracting out of registration functions: fees

(1) Regulations may make provision about the charging of fees where an authorised person exercises a function of a traffic commissioner in relation to an application specified in subsection (2).

(2) Those applications are—

(a) an application under section 6 of this Act for the registration of a relevant service,

(b) an application under section 6 of this Act for the variation of the registration of a service that, as varied, would be or continue to be a relevant service, and

(c) an application under section 6 of this Act for the cancellation of the registration of a relevant service.

(3) Regulations under this section may allow or require the authorised person to charge fees in respect of the application to which the function relates.

(4) The regulations may—

(a) specify the fees chargeable, or

(b) make provision about the setting of fees by the authorised person, including provision about determining the amounts of such fees.

(5) The regulations may include provision about—

(a) who must pay the fees and at what times, and

(b) whether the fees are payable in one sum or in instalments.

(6) The regulations may provide that, if a fee or instalment of a fee due under the regulations has not been paid, the authorised person may decline to proceed with an application referred to in subsection (2) to which the fee or instalment relates until the fee or instalment is paid.

(7) The regulations may make provision about how amounts received in respect of fees charged under the regulations are to be applied.

(8) Provision made by virtue of subsection (7) may include—

(a) provision for such amounts not to be payable to the traffic commissioner, and

(b) provision that such amounts are to be paid, or not to be paid, into the Consolidated Fund.

(9) The regulations may provide that fees are not to be charged under section 52 of the 1981 Act (as applied by section 126 of this Act) in respect of the applications referred to in subsection (2).

(10) In this section—

"authorised person", in relation to a function of a traffic commissioner, means a person authorised to exercise that function by virtue of an authorisation given in accordance with an order under section 69 of the Deregulation and Contracting Out Act 1994;

"relevant service" means a service which has stopping places only in England;

"service" has the meaning given in section 6(1)."

Bus companies: authorities in England

22 Bus companies: limitation of powers of authorities in England

(1) A relevant authority may not, in exercise of any of its powers, form a company for the purpose of providing a local service.

(2) Subsection (1) applies whether the relevant authority is acting alone or with any other person.

(3) In this section—

"company" has the same meaning as in the Companies Acts (see sections 1(1) and 2(1) of the Companies Act 2006);

"form a company" is to be construed in accordance with section 7 of the Companies Act 2006;

"local service" has the same meaning as in the Transport Act 1985 (see section 2 of that Act);

"Passenger Transport Executive", in relation to an integrated transport area in England or a combined authority area, means the body which is the Executive in relation to that area for the purposes of Part 2 of the Transport Act 1968;

"relevant authority" means—

(a) a county council in England;

(b) a district council in England;
(c) a combined authority established under section 103 of the Local Democracy, Economic Development and Construction Act 2009;
(d) an Integrated Transport Authority for an integrated transport area in England;
(e) a Passenger Transport Executive for—
  (i) an integrated transport area in England, or
  (ii) a combined authority area.

General

23 Power to make consequential provision

(1) The Secretary of State may by regulations make such provision as appears to the Secretary of State to be appropriate in consequence of any provision made by or under this Act.

(2) The power conferred by subsection (1) includes power to amend, repeal, revoke or otherwise modify—
  (a) an Act passed before or in the same Session as this Act, or
  (b) an instrument made under an Act before the regulations come into force.

(3) Regulations under this section must be made by statutory instrument.

(4) A statutory instrument which contains (whether alone or with other provision) regulations under this section that amend or repeal a provision of an Act may not be made unless a draft of the instrument has been laid before, and approved by a resolution of, each House of Parliament.

(5) A statutory instrument which contains any other regulations under this section is subject to annulment in pursuance of a resolution of either House of Parliament.

24 Power to make transitional, transitory or saving provision

(1) The Secretary of State may by regulations make such transitional, transitory or saving provision as the Secretary of State considers appropriate in connection with the coming into force of any provision of this Act.

(2) The regulations may in particular make provision about ticketing schemes under section 135 of the Transport Act 2000 relating to areas in England that exist immediately before the day on which section 7 of this Act comes into force.

(3) The regulations may include provision for treating such ticketing schemes as made under section 134C of the Transport Act 2000 (inserted by section 7 of this Act).

(4) Regulations under this section must be made by statutory instrument.

(5) A statutory instrument which contains regulations under this section is subject to annulment in pursuance of a resolution of either House of Parliament.

25 Extent

(1) This Act extends to England and Wales only, subject to the following subsections.

(2) Section 17(1) to (4) extend to England and Wales and Scotland.

(3) Section 17(6) extends to Scotland only.

(4) Sections 23 to 27 extend to England and Wales and Scotland.

26 Commencement

(1) The following come into force on the day on which this Act is passed—

- (a) section 23;
- (b) section 24;
- (c) section 25;
- (d) this section;
- (e) section 27.

(2) Section 17 comes into force on such day as the Secretary of State may by regulations made by statutory instrument appoint.

(3) The remaining provisions of this Act—

- (a) come into force, for the purposes of making regulations or orders, on the day on which this Act is passed, and
- (b) come into force, for remaining purposes, at the end of the period of two months beginning with the day on which this Act is passed.

27 Short title

This Act may be cited as the Bus Services Act 2017.

SCHEDULES

SCHEDULE 1

Section 2

FURTHER AMENDMENTS: ADVANCED QUALITY PARTNERSHIP SCHEMES

Transport Act 1985 (c. 67)

1 The Transport Act 1985 is amended as follows.

2 (1) Section 6 (registration of local services) is amended as follows.

(2) In subsection (2A), in paragraph (a)—

(a) after "section" insert "113D(1) or";

(b) for "(quality" substitute "(advanced quality partnership schemes and quality".

3 (1) Section 6A (applications for registration where restrictions are in force) is amended as follows.

(2) In subsection (1), in paragraph (a)—

(a) after "section" insert "113D(1) or";

(b) after "case of" insert "an advanced quality partnership scheme or".

(3) In subsection (8), in paragraph (c), after "section" insert "113J(4) or (5) or".

(4) In subsection (12)—

(a) at the appropriate place insert—

""advanced quality partnership scheme" means a scheme under section 113C of the Transport Act 2000;";

(b) for the definition of "registration criteria" substitute—

""registration criteria"—

(a) in relation to an advanced quality partnership scheme, means the criteria specified in the scheme by virtue of section 113D(3) of the Transport Act 2000;

(b) in relation to a quality partnership scheme, means the criteria specified in the scheme by virtue of section 114(3C) of the Transport Act 2000;";

(c) in the definition of "relevant operator", in paragraph (a), after "section" insert "113J(4) or (5) or".

4 In section 26 (conditions attached to a PSV operator's licence), in subsection (1), in paragraph (b), after "section or section" insert "113J(4) or (5),".

5 In section 82 (bus stations: restrictions on discriminatory practices, etc), in subsection (4A), in the words before paragraph (a), after "to" insert "an advanced quality partnership scheme or".

Transport Act 2000 (c. 38)

6 The Transport Act 2000 (as amended by the Local Transport Act 2008) is amended as follows.

7 (1) Section 114 (quality partnership schemes) is amended as follows.

(2) In subsection (1), at the end insert "(but this is subject to subsection (1A)).

(3) After subsection (1) insert—

"(1A) A local transport authority whose area is in England may exercise the power to make a quality partnership scheme only if—

(a) they are acting jointly with one or more other local transport authorities, and

(b) at least one of those other local transport authorities is an authority whose area is in Wales."

8 (1) Section 153 (competition test: functions and agreements relating to buses) is amended as follows.

(2) In subsection (1), in paragraph (a), after "to" insert "advanced quality partnership schemes,".

(3) In subsection (3), in the definition of "voluntary agreement", after "under" insert "sections 113C to 113O (advanced quality partnership schemes), or under".

9 In section 155 (sanctions), in subsection (1), in paragraph (b), after "section", in the second place it occurs, insert "113J(4) or (5),".

10 In section 162 (interpretation of Part 2), in subsection (1), at the appropriate place insert—

"“advanced quality partnership scheme” is to be construed in accordance with section 113C(2),".

11 (1) Schedule 10 (competition test: functions and agreements relating to buses) is amended as follows.

(2) In paragraph 1 (functions to which Part 1 of Schedule 10 applies)—

(a) in sub-paragraph (1), before paragraph (a) insert—

"(za) making and varying advanced quality partnership schemes,";

(b) in sub-paragraph (2), before paragraph (a) insert—

"(za) in the case of the function of making or varying an advanced quality partnership scheme, once notice of a proposal to make or vary it has been given under section 113G(1),".

(3) In paragraph 12 (enforcement of decisions of Competition and Markets Authority), in sub-paragraph (2)(b), after "varying" insert "an advanced quality partnership scheme,".

(4) In paragraph 17 (interpretation of Part 2 of Schedule 10), in sub-paragraph (5)(c), at the beginning insert "an advanced quality partnership scheme,".

SCHEDULE 2

Section 6

FURTHER AMENDMENTS: FRANCHISING SCHEMES

Transport Act 1985 (c. 67)

1 The Transport Act 1985 is amended as follows.

2 In section 6 (registration of local services)—

(a) in subsection (2B) (registration in quality contract scheme cases), in paragraph (a), after "force" insert "in relation to an area in Wales";

(b) in subsection (7A) (variation of registration in quality contract scheme cases), in paragraph (a), after "force" insert "in relation to an area in Wales".

3 (1) Section 26 (conditions attached to a PSV operator's licence) is amended as follows.

(2) In subsection (1) (circumstances in which conditions may be imposed), in paragraph (b), after "118(4)" insert ", 123J(3)".

(3) In subsection (1)(bza), after "section" insert "123X(7)(c),".

(4) In subsection (1), after paragraph (ba) (and the "or" following it) insert—

"(baa) the operator has failed to take all reasonable steps to comply with a requirement imposed under section 143A of the Transport Act 2000; or"."

4 In section 66 (powers of councils to run bus undertakings), in subsection (1), for "and to section" substitute "and to sections 123O and".

Transport Act 2000 (c. 38)

5 The Transport Act 2000 (as amended by the Local Transport Act 2008) is amended as follows.

6 In the heading preceding section 124, after "schemes" insert "in Wales".

7 (1) Section 124 (quality contracts schemes) is amended as follows.

(2) In subsection (1), after "authority", in the first place it occurs, insert "for an area in Wales".

(3) Omit subsections (1A) and (1B).

(4) In subsection (2)—

(a) at the end of paragraph (a), insert "and";

(b) in paragraph (b), omit "in the case of a scheme for an area in Wales,";

(c) omit paragraph (c) and the "and" preceding it.

(5) Omit subsection (2A).

(6) In subsection (9)—

(a) after "authority", in the first place it occurs, insert "for an area in Wales";

(b) after "another" insert "such".

(7) Omit subsection (9A).

(8) Omit subsections (11) to (13).

8 In section 125 (notice and consultation requirements)—

(a) in subsection (1)—

(i) at the end of paragraph (b), insert "and";

(ii) omit paragraph (d) and the "and" preceding it;

(b) in subsection (1A)(b), omit "or, as the case may be, (1A)";

(c) in subsection (3)(e), omit "if the proposed scheme relates to an area in Wales,".

9 In section 126 (approval of proposed schemes for areas in Wales), omit subsection (A1).

10 Omit sections 126A to 126E (QCS boards for schemes for areas in England).

11 In section 127 (making of scheme)—

(a) in subsection (1), omit paragraph (a);

(b) in subsection (1)(b), omit "in the case of a scheme for an area in Wales,";

(c) omit subsection (1A);

(d) in subsection (1B), omit paragraph (a) and the "and" following it;

(e) in subsection (10), omit "(1A),".

12 Omit sections 127A and 127B (appeals: schemes for areas in England).

13 In section 131A (continuation of schemes for further periods)—

(a) in subsection (2)—

(i) in paragraph (a), omit ", if the scheme is for an area in Wales, or";

(ii) omit paragraph (b);

(b) omit subsection (4);

(c) in subsection (5)—

(i) in paragraph (b), omit "or, as the case may be, paragraphs (b) to (d) of section 124(1A)";

(ii) in paragraph (c), omit "or, as the case may be, (1A)".

14 Omit section 131C (continuation of schemes for areas in England: procedure).

15 In section 131E (appeals where proposed continuation considered exempt), in subsection (13), omit the words from "If" to "Wales,".

16 Omit section 131F (appeals where proposed continuation considered non-exempt).

17 In section 132 (variation or revocation of scheme)—

(a) in subsection (2), omit "or those set out in subsection (1A)(a) to (d) of that section";

(b) in subsection (4A), omit paragraph (b);

(c) in subsection (5), omit paragraphs (a) to (c) and the "or" following paragraph (c);

(d) omit subsections (6) to (8).

18 In section 132A (appeals where proposed variation considered exempt), in subsection (12), omit the words from "If" to "Wales,".

19 In section 132B (exemption from section 132 for specific variations directed by Tribunal), omit subsection (1)(a).

20 In section 133 (regulations about schemes)—

(a) in subsection (1)(b), omit "for areas in Wales";

(b) omit subsection (1)(bb) and (bc);
(c) in subsection (2)(e), omit "for areas in Wales";
(d) omit subsection (2)(ef) to (ei);
(e) omit subsection (3)(a);
(f) omit subsection (4)(b).

21 (1) Section 155 (sanctions imposed by traffic commissioners) is amended as follows.

(2) In subsection (1) (when sanctions may be imposed), in paragraph (ba), after "section" insert "123X(7)(c),".

(3) After subsection (1) insert—

"(1ZA) Where a traffic commissioner is satisfied that—

(a) a person has operated a local service in contravention of section 123J(3) of this Act, and
(b) in operating the local service, the person has failed to take all reasonable precautions and to exercise all due diligence to avoid contravening section 123J(3) of this Act,

the traffic commissioner may make one or more orders under subsection (1A)(a) or (d)."

(4) After subsection (1ZB) (inserted by Schedule 4) insert—

"(1ZC) Where a traffic commissioner is satisfied that the operator of a local service has failed to take all reasonable steps to comply with a requirement imposed under section 143A of this Act, the traffic commissioner may make one or more orders under subsection (1A)(a) or (d)."

22 (1) Section 160 (regulations and orders under Part 2) is amended as follows.

(2) In subsection (2), after "than" insert "regulations under section 123A(4)".

(3) After subsection (2) insert—

"(2A) A statutory instrument containing regulations under section 123A(4) shall not be made unless a draft of the instrument has been laid before, and approved by a resolution of, each House of Parliament."

23 (1) Section 162 (interpretation of Part 2) is amended as follows.

(2) In subsection (1) (specific terms), at the appropriate place insert—

"“effective time”, in relation to a local service contract, has the meaning given by section 123J(7),";

"“franchising authority” has the meaning given by section 123A(4),";

"“franchising scheme” is to be construed in accordance with section 123A(3),";

"“interim service” has the meaning given by section 123O,";

"“local service contract” has the meaning given by section 123A(5),";

"“mayoral combined authority” has the meaning given by section 107A of the Local Democracy, Economic Development and Construction Act 2009,";

"“scheme sub-area” has the meaning given by section 123H,";

"“service permit” has the meaning given by section 123P,".

(3) In subsection (1), in the definition of "appropriate national authority", omit paragraph (a) (meaning for schemes relating to areas in England).

(4) In subsection (1), omit the definition of "QCS board".

(5) In subsection (4) (interpretation of references to Integrated Transport Authorities), omit the following entries—

"section 124(4)(a), (5) and (7),";
"section 127(3A),";
"section 127A(7),";
"section 130,";
"section 131,";
"section 132C,";
"section 132D,".

Local Transport Act 2008 (c. 26)

24 The Local Transport Act 2008 is amended as follows.

25 Omit sections 22 to 25 (QCS boards in England).

26 Omit section 27 (appeals against making of quality contract schemes in England).

27 Omit section 33 (continuation of quality contract schemes for areas in England).

28 Omit section 36 (appeals where proposed continuation of scheme considered non-exempt).

SCHEDULE 3

Section 8

FURTHER AMENDMENTS: ADVANCED TICKETING SCHEMES

Transport Act 1985 (c. 67)

1 The Transport Act 1985 is amended as follows.

2 In section 26 (conditions attached to a PSV operator's licence), in subsection (1)(ba), after "section" insert "134F,".

Transport Act 2000 (c. 38)

3 The Transport Act 2000 (as amended by the Local Transport Act 2008) is amended as follows.

4 (1) Section 135 (joint and through ticketing schemes) is amended as follows.

(2) In subsection (1), at the end insert—

"(but this is subject to subsection (1A))."

(3) After subsection (1) insert—

"(1A) A local transport authority whose area is in England may exercise the power to make a ticketing scheme only if—

(a) they are acting jointly with one or more other local transport authorities, and

(b) at least one of those other local transport authorities is an authority whose area is in Wales."

5 In section 153 (competition test: functions and agreements relating to buses), in subsection (1)(a), after "partnership schemes," insert "advanced ticketing schemes,".

6 In section 155 (sanctions), in subsection (1)(c), after "section" insert "134F,".

7 (1) Section 162 (interpretation of Part 2) is amended as follows.

(2) In subsection (1), in the definition of "connecting rail or tram service" for "service"" substitute

"""service"—

(a) in relation to an advanced ticketing scheme, has the meaning given by section 134C(3), and

(b) in relation to a ticketing scheme,".

(3) In subsection (1), at the appropriate place insert—

"""advanced ticketing scheme" is to be construed in accordance with section 134C(3),".

8 (1) Schedule 10 (competition test: functions and agreements relating to buses) is amended as follows.

(2) In paragraph 1 (functions to which Part 1 of Schedule 10 applies)—

(a) in sub-paragraph (1), after paragraph (a) insert—

"(aa) making and varying advanced ticketing schemes,";

(b) in sub-paragraph (2), after paragraph (a) insert—

"(aa) in the case of the function of making or varying an advanced ticketing scheme, once notice of a proposal to make or vary it has been given under section 134D(1),".

(3) In paragraph 12 (enforcement of decisions of Competition and Markets Authority), in sub-paragraph (2)(b), after "partnership scheme" insert ", an advanced ticketing scheme".

SCHEDULE 4

Section 15

FURTHER AMENDMENTS: ENHANCED PARTNERSHIP PLANS AND SCHEMES

Transport Act 1985 (c. 67)

1 The Transport Act 1985 is amended as follows.

2 (1) Section 7 (application of traffic regulation conditions to services registered under section 6) is amended as follows.

(2) After subsection (3) insert—

"(3A) Traffic regulation conditions may not be expressed to apply to an area to which an enhanced partnership scheme under section 138A of the Transport Act 2000 relates."

(3) After subsection (14) insert—

"(14A) Where an enhanced partnership scheme under section 138A of the Transport Act 2000 comes into operation as regards an area, any traffic regulation condition expressed to apply in an area that consists of or includes the area to which the scheme relates ceases at that time to apply in the area to which the scheme relates.

(14B) A traffic commissioner may accordingly vary or revoke a traffic regulation condition (without a request being made)."

3 (1) Section 26 (conditions attached to a PSV operator's licence) is amended as follows.

(2) In subsection (1) (when conditions may be attached), in paragraph (b), for "or 129(1)(b)" substitute ", 129(1)(b) or 138J(9)".

(3) In subsection (1)(bza), after "134B(7)(c)" insert "or 138S(7)(c)".

(4) In subsection (1)(baa) (inserted by Schedule 2), after "143A" insert "or 143B".

Transport Act 2000 (c. 38)

4 The Transport Act 2000 (as amended by the Local Transport Act 2008) is amended as follows.

5 In section 153 (competition test: functions and agreements relating to buses), in subsection (1)(a) (applying tests in relation to the exercise of functions relating to quality partnership schemes, etc), after "ticketing schemes" insert ", enhanced partnership schemes".

6 (1) Section 155 (sanctions relating to Part 2 of the Act) is amended as follows.

(2) In subsection (1)(b), for "or 129(1)(b)" substitute ", 129(1)(b) or 138J(9)".

(3) In subsection (1)(ba), after "134B(7)(c)" insert "or 138S(7)(c)".

(4) After subsection (1ZA) (inserted by Schedule 2) insert—

"(1ZB) Where a traffic commissioner is satisfied that—

(a) a person has operated a local service in contravention of section 138J(9) of this Act, and

(b) in operating the local service, the person has failed to take all reasonable precautions and to exercise all due diligence to avoid contravening section 138J(9) of this Act,

the traffic commissioner may make one or more orders under subsection (1A)(a) or (d)."

(5) After subsection (1ZC) (inserted by Schedule 2) insert—

"(1ZD) Where a traffic commissioner is satisfied that the operator of a local service has failed to take all reasonable steps to comply with a requirement imposed under section 143B the traffic commissioner may make one or more orders under subsection (1A)(a) or (d)."

7 (1) Section 160 (regulations and orders under Part 2) is amended as follows.

(2) In subsection (2), after "regulations under section 123A(4)" (inserted by Schedule 2 to this Act) insert ", 138F(10), 138G(9)".

(3) In subsection (2A) (inserted by Schedule 2 to this Act), after "regulations under section 123A(4)" insert ", 138F(10), 138G(9)".

8 In section 162 (interpretation of Part 2 of the Act), in subsection (1), at the appropriate place insert—

""enhanced partnership plan" and "enhanced partnership scheme" have the meaning given by section 138A,".

9 (1) Schedule 10 (competition test: functions and agreements relating to buses) is amended as follows.

(2) In paragraph 1 (functions to which Part 1 of Schedule 10 applies)—

(a) after sub-paragraph (1)(b) (and before the "and") insert—

"(ba) making and varying enhanced partnership schemes,";

(b) after sub-paragraph (2)(b) (and before the "and") insert—

"(ba) in the case of the function of making or varying an enhanced partnership scheme, once notice of a proposal to make or vary it has been given under section 138F(1) or 138L(1),".

(3) In paragraph 12 (enforcement of decisions of Competition and Markets Authority), in sub-paragraph (2)(b), for "or a ticketing scheme" substitute ", a ticketing scheme or an enhanced partnership scheme".

(4) In paragraph 17 (interpretation of Part 2 of Schedule 10), in sub-paragraph (5)(c), after "scheme" insert ", an enhanced partnership scheme".

Adapted and published by GRANGIS under the OGL Licence 3.0.

www.nationalarchives.gov.uk/doc/open-government-licence/version/3/

GRANGIS - UK PUBLISHING 2022.
Thank you for taking the time to leave us a review regarding this version

★★★★★

For further inquiries, contact us at:
www.grangis.com / contact@grangis.com

www.ingramcontent.com/pod-product-compliance
Lightning Source LLC
LaVergne TN
LVHW060213210926
848481LV00008B/2728